THE
LAST
NATSARIM

Ambassadors of the Reign of Yahusha

Lew White

Also available as Kindle eBook at amazon.com

Lew White, author
www.torahzone.net
www.fossilizedcustoms.com

Copyright © 2019-2020 by Lew White
Published by Torah Institute

Available exclusively from Amazon.com
Visit Lew White's Author's Page

**Subscribe to author's youtube video channels
Lew White & Torah Institute**

CONTENTS

Page 10	What Were The First Natsarim Like?
Page 11	Turn The World Upside-Down With A Name
Page 13	PAUL AT THE AREOPAGUS
Page 16, 86	WHAT WAS THE OLD COVENANT?
Page 22	PAUL – RINGLEADER OF THE NATSARIM
Page 23	SCROLL OF REMEMBRANCE
Page 24	TEACHING AUTHORITY
Page 26, 36	WHAT IS EISEGESIS?
Page 29	JESUIT – NATSARIM CONVERSATION
Page 38, 70	CHRISTOGRAMS
Page 39	What Is A Worship Service?
Page 42	Why Earth Will Be Burned
Page 43	FISCUS JUDAICUS
Page 44	Epiphanius Headmaster CSA/Didascalia - 4th Century
Page 46	OTHER NAMES FOR NATSARIM
Page 47	ORIGEN – Self-Castrated Headmaster
Page 47	CHRISTIANOS – BEING CALLED AN IDIOT
Page 50	We Have Inherited Hindu Behavior
Page 53	HEBREW LANGUAGE - PROOF
Page 54	PERSECUTION / MASSACRE

Page 62, 102	**BARUK HABA BASHEM YAHUAH**
Page 68	**ORIGIN OF WORD GOD**
Page 72	**How To Recognize Idolatry**
Page 73	**ANIMAL HOUSE** - NO ZODIAC WITCHCRAFT
Page 74	**REDEMPTION PLAN**
Page 78	**LOVE TRAINING**
Page 83, 93	**RACIAL BIGOTRY**
Page 100	**Vatican Forbids The Name Yahuah**
Page 116	**The Spirit of Error** (NATSARIM vs. CHRISTIAN)
Page 125	**DIGEST THE IDIOMS**
Page 127	**GLOSSARY OF HEBREW TERMS**
Page 137	**LETTER CHART**

Last Natsarim: *First-fruits of the End Times*
The last Natsarim are a remnant being guided by the Spirit of Yahusha to awaken many to uprightness and be restored to favor. As prophesied at Danial 12, many are being awakened.
We are the ***hidden arrow*** in Yahuah's quiver for the last days, the ***first-fruits*** of many to come. Yaqub (Yisharal) is awakening:

"Listen to Me, O coastlands, and hear, you peoples from afar! Yahuah has called Me from the womb, from My mother's belly He has caused My Name to be remembered. And He made My mouth like a sharp sword, in the shadow of His hand He hid Me, and made Me a polished shaft. In His quiver He hid Me." And He said to Me, 'You are My Servant, O Yisharal, in whom I am adorned.' And I said, 'I have labored in vain, I have spent my strength for emptiness, and in vain. But my lawfulness is with Yahuah, and my work with my Alahim.' " And now said Yahuah – who formed Me from the womb to be His Servant,

to bring Yaqub back to Him, though Yisharal is not gathered to Him, yet I am esteemed in the eyes of Yahuah, and My Alahim has been My strength – and He says, "Shall it be a small matter for You to be My Servant to raise up the tribes of Yaqub, and to bring back the preserved ones of Yisharal? And I shall give You as a light to the guyim (nations), to be My deliverance to the ends of the arets!" Thus said Yahuah, the Redeemer of Yisharal, their Qodesh One, to the despised, to the loathed One of the nation, to the Servant of rulers, "Kings shall see and arise, rulers also shall bow themselves, because of Yahuah who is steadfast, the Qodesh One of Yisharal. And He has chosen You!" Thus said Yahuah, "In a favorable time I shall answer You, and in the yom of deliverance I shall help You – and I guard You and give You for a covenant of the people, to restore the arets, to cause them to inherit the ruined inheritances, to say to the prisoners, 'Go out,' to those who are in darkness, 'Show yourselves!'"
YashaYahu (Is.) 49:1-9

We are sent to those sitting in darkness.

NATSARIM is a plural form of the Hebrew word **natsar**.
It can mean *watchmen* or *branches* depending on how it is used in a sentence. It refers to **those who are branches of the teachings of Yahusha.** They abide in His Word, obeying the Commandments of Yahuah and teaching the world the true Name of Yahusha (see Revelation 12:17). The term **watchmen** is found in English translations at YirmeYahu (Jer.) 31:6, a prophecy of Natsarim arising in the end times, crying out an invitation.
Yahusha is regenerating us to be ambassadors of His reign:
"For there shall be a yom [day] *when the Natsarim cry on Mount Afraim, 'Arise, and let us go up to Tsiun, to Yahuah our Alahim.'"* - YirmeYahu (Jer.) 31:6 BYNV Kindle eBook
When every eye of mankind sees Yahusha coming back to rule here on Earth from the darkness of space, they will be so terrified. They will want the mountains to hide them from His Kabod (brilliance), and the last Natsarim will be here to tell them this:

"And it shall be said in that yom, 'See, this is our Alahim.

We have waited for Him, and He saves us. This is Yahuah, we have waited for Him, let us be glad and rejoice in His deliverance.'" – YashaYahu (Is.) 25:9 BYNV

THE LAST NATSARIM ARE HERE

Yahusha has placed His seal us, and is preparing to separate us from those He has decided to pour out the wrath of His displeasure on a day He has set to burn the entire Earth (arets).

Paul spoke of the Day of Yahuah to the Greek philosophers as he observed all the altars they had built to serve their many deities. Hearing of a man resurrecting from the dead, they compelled him to stand before the nobles of Areopagus, to whom Paul announced:

"Truly, then, having overlooked these times of ignorance, Alahim now commands all men everywhere to repent, because He has set a yom on which He is going to judge the world in obedience by a Man whom He has appointed, having given proof of this to all by raising Him from the dead." – Acts 17:30-31

Over 400 judges heard Paul say this, and some of them believed what he said.

Prophecy Describes Yahusha's Return

Scripture refers to a second, and greater deliverance that overshadows the first Exodus from Egypt. Prior to the Babylonian Captivity, YirmeYahu (Jer.) wrote of it extensively. Yahuah brought out the tribes of Israel from Egypt, along with a mixed multitude that engrafted into the nation. There is a final Exodus just ahead, at the end of the Great Tribulation (distress).

This distress is also known as *Yaqub's trouble*. (YirmeYahu 30:7)
The Second Exodus will be so incredible and miraculous, the first Exodus will pale by comparison:

"'Therefore see, the days are coming,' declares Yahuah, 'when it is no longer said, "Yahuah lives who brought up the children of Yisharal from the land of Mitsrayim," but, "Yahuah lives who brought up the children of Yisharal from the land of the north and from all the lands where He had driven them." For I shall bring them back into their land I gave to their fathers. 'See, I am sending for many fishermen,' declares Yahuah, 'and they shall fish them. And after that I shall send for many hunters, and they shall hunt them from every mountain and every hill, and out of the holes of the rocks.'" – YirmeYahu 16:14-16

The following describes the second-coming of Yahusha, and the Second Exodus to **deliver** His sealed ones from the **king of Babel**: YirmeYahu (Jeremiah) 23:3-8:

**"'Therefore I shall gather the remnant of My flock out of all the lands where I have driven them, and shall bring them back to their fold. And they shall bear and increase.
And I shall raise up shepherds over them, and they shall feed them. And they shall fear no more, nor be discouraged, nor shall they be lacking,' declares Yahuah. 'See, the days are coming,' declares Yahuah, 'when I shall raise for Daud a Branch of righteousness, and a Sovereign shall reign and act wisely, and shall do right-ruling and righteousness in the earth.
In His days Yahudah shall be saved, and Yisharal dwell safely. And this is His Name whereby He shall be called:
Yahuah is our Righteousness.**
    (Transliterated in Hebrew: **Yahuah Tsediqenu**; Yahusha's new Name)
**Therefore, see, the days are coming,' declares Yahuah, 'when they shall say no more, "As Yahuah lives who brought up the children of Yisharal out of the land of Mitsrayim," but, "As Yahuah lives who brought up and led the seed of the house of Yisharal out of the land of the north and from all the lands where I had driven them." And they shall dwell on their own soil.
See, I am bringing them from the land of the north, and shall gather them from the ends of the earth, among them the blind and the lame, those with child and those in labor, together – a great assembly returning here.'"**

Read Ps 80, keeping in mind it is the cry of Afraim.
More of what YirmeYahu has to say can be studied here:
www.fossilizedcustoms.com/secondexodus.html

Many are being sealed with the true Name, Yahusha.
Reapers are coming to remove all things detestable to Yahuah. Traditions always wrestle against the Truth. One of the most serious strongholds is the false name, Jesus, invented by men less than 500 years ago. Our fathers inherited *nothing* but falsehood, and the translations removed the key of knowledge: the **Name**.

GOOGLE: YAHUSHA

Natsarim understand, wanting to be obedient servants, and in the eyes of Yahusha, we are the greatest because we *serve*.
Our humble behavior is the fruit of His presence showing itself in the love we have for one another, and even our enemies.
Proverbs 28:4 says, **"Those forsaking Turah praise the wrong, but those guarding Turah strive against them."**
[Turah means *instruction*]

We imitate Yahusha because we are His ashah, His wife.
The **branches** of the teachings of Yahusha have multiplied on Earth in recent years. The first Natsarim wrote many warning letters for the world to heed and obey, and became a threat to the dragon and his authority. The book you are reading is about a marriage between Yahuah and a chosen ashah (wife, maiden). The dragon has deceived the whole world, but a remnant has been awakened in the last days. Just as the first followers of Yahusha were the first Natsarim (Acts 24:5), We are the **LAST NATSARIM**.
The Natsarim are the ashah of Yahusha, His remnant bride also known as *first-fruits*, or wise virgins.
We are part of a living contract, and we have been purchased by the blood of the Ruach ha Qodesh, Who is Yahusha!
(See Acts 20:28)

Revelation 12:16-17 speaks of the Natsarim as the ashah:
"And the arets helped the ashah, and the arets opened its mouth and swallowed up the river which the dragon had spewed out of his mouth. And the dragon was enraged with

the ashah, and he went to fight with the remnant of her seed, those guarding the commands of Yahuah and possessing the witness of Yahusha Mashiak." Rev. 12:16-17 BYNV

We are the first-fruits, the remnant, also called the bride (ashah) of Yahusha. We are sealed by His Name. (see Revelation 14)
The last Natsarim are the ambassadors of the reign of Yahusha, and appear to be common vessels, but contain a precious treasure: The living presence of the Creator of the universe.
We are Natsarim, the repairers of the breach.
Yahuah is looking for His obedient wife, the maiden that is waiting for Him. Most have no idea their teachers have kept them from knowing Yahusha, and Who He really is.

We are announcing the reign of Yahusha, and the fall of the reign of Babel
Repent! For the reign of Yahuah draws near!
And we are announcing the words of Psalm 118:26
BARUK HABA BASHEM YAHUAH
A literal translation into English:
Blessed is the one Coming In the Name of Yahuah

The Silk Road trade route brought Nimrod's culture to the Middle East & went wild.
Before Yahusha returns, His Natsarim are here to warn you.

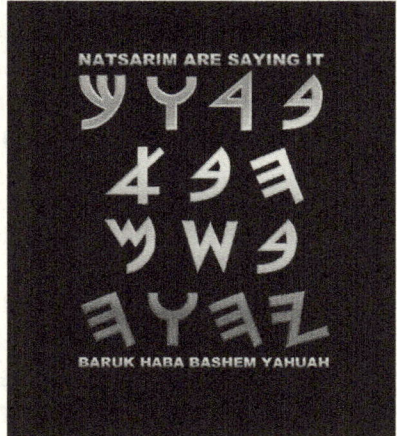

Backprint on shirt available at Yahusha World Garments, Amazon.com

The vast majority of deceived people here in the last days have inherited lies and futility from their fathers. They are ever-learning, but never able to gain a knowledge of the Truth. We Natsarim are suddenly appearing to urge all men to be restored to favor.
Most people first hearing the Truth are too drunk on men's teachings to understand, but we stay at out post in order to turn many to righteousness. We keep appealing to the lost and those held in strongholds so we will be found doing, not hearing only.
The Spirit / Ruach of prophecy is the testimony of Yahusha, speaking through us. We don't know what we will say until the moment He chooses to give us the words others need to hear.
Galatians 2:20 tells us,

"I no longer live, but Mashiak lives in me."

Hear Him in His Natsarim.

What Were The First Natsarim Like?
Let's look at some of their writings here to see how they lived:

"We are witnesses of these things, and so is the Ruach haQodesh, Whom Alahim has given to those who obey Him."
- Acts 5:32

Another one of the first Natsarim wrote:
"But there also came to be false prophets among the people, as also among you there shall be false teachers, who shall secretly bring in destructive heresies, and deny the Master who bought them, bringing swift destruction on themselves. And many shall follow their destructive ways, because of whom the way of truth shall be evil spoken of, and in greed, with fabricated words, they shall use you for gain. From of old their judgment does not linger, and their destruction does not slumber." 2Kefa / Peter 2:1-3

The first Natsarim held to completely different teachings than we see practiced by Christians. The last Natsarim are being awakened, and can see the seraphim about to fulfill Malaki 4. Ask your pastor if they know the *message of AliYahu* mentioned in that chapter, and why they haven't told you about it. AliYahu asked the teaching authority which they should serve, Yahuah or Baal. The people shouted,
"Yahuah! He is Alahim! -- Yahuah! He is Alahim!" 1Kings 18:39

Don't let the servants of **Bel** (LORD) get away with their deceptions. Yahuah said His people will know His Name. Not Bel, Belzebub, or Izabel. The Mt. Karmel controversy over the Name should be over by now!

"He who turns his ear away from hearing the Turah, even his prayer is an abomination." - Proverbs 28:9

The world did not know Yahusha because they did not know Yahuah. Our sect was despised everywhere, because it was a threat to the teaching authorities, *the fake workers who wanted the vineyard for themselves.* The present day Natsarim are watching the entrenched Christian authorities saying the same things about us that were said then: **"'And we think it right to hear from you what you think, for indeed, concerning this sect, we know that it is spoken against everywhere.'"** - Acts 28:22

We Turn The World Upside-Down With A Name
We come in the Name of Yahusha, and it's turning the world upside-down again. The Name people have accepted is being challenged by the Truth, just as it was in the days we first appeared:
"But the Yahudim who did not believe, having become envious, took some of the belyial *[wicked]* **men from the market-place, and gathering a mob, set all the city in an uproar and came upon the house of Iasouos, and were seeking to bring them out to the people. But not finding them, they dragged Iasouos and some of the brothers to the city rulers, crying out, 'They who have turned the world upside down have come here too, whom Iasouos has received. And all of them are acting contrary to the teachings of Kaisar, saying there is another king, *Yahusha.*'"** – Acts 17:5-7

The Christogram **IESV** from the Latin Vulgate produced the form ***JESUS*** and the Islamic ***ISA***. Neither are based on the real Name, spoken and written in Hebrew, yod-hay-uau-shin-ayin (YAHUSHA). The first Natsarim followers didn't know anyone named JESUS. The last Natsarim are here now, and warning the teachers first, and the crowds are all watching them try to explain their traditions.
We are the first-fruits, bearing the final message of AliYahu (Malaki 4:1-6). Have I become your enemy, having spoken Truth to you?

The false teachers stand by without lifting up their voices to warn the crowds about practicing pagan fertility traditions adopted long ago. Missionary adaptation, or syncretism, are two terms to look up on the Internet, and will reveal how history has been revised to accommodate the beliefs of the unconverted heathens. Now the whole world has turned aside to *myths*. What could possibly go wrong? On the Day of Yahuah, everyone will find out.

TURNED ASIDE TO MYTHS
NOT BEARING SOUND DOCTRINE TEACHERS INCREASE CHAOS
WHAT COULD POSSIBLY GO WRONG?

2 TIMOTHY 4:1-6   MALAKI 4:1-6

What Myths, Who's Teaching Them, And What Could Possibly Go Wrong
Sound doctrines are all now replaced by traditions of men. Futility, lies, and myths have filled the earth with customs people embrace as familiar, and the Truth has become thought of as evil. Paul wrote of these things to Timothy: **"Proclaim the Word! Be urgent in season, out of season. Correct, warn, appeal, with all patience and teaching. For there shall be a time when they shall not bear sound teaching, but according to their own desires, they shall heap up for themselves teachers tickling the ear, and they shall indeed turn their ears away from the Truth, and be turned aside to myths."** - 2Timothy 4:2-4

A myth is a widely-held belief, among these are sacraments, holy water, transubstantiation, Sun-day, Trinities, celibacy, image worship, popes, nuns, monks, steeples, obelisks, wreaths, lent, chants, special days, prayers to the dead, indulgences, pilgrimages, stigmatas, Easter egg hunts, Dec. 25th Solstice birth, Santa, elves, trees in homes, monstrances, bells, and all forms of fertility patterns of Babel. The **King of Babel** has deceived them. Luke reports for us in Acts about many events spanning about 32 years after the death and resurrection of Yahusha. He describes many of the challenges faced by his fellow-traveler and convert we know today as Paul. Paul was *formerly* known as Shaul, who had been given authority by the Sanhedrin to arrest the first Natsarim

(branches) in the assemblies found to be uttering Yahuah's Name, which they called *blasphemy*. Shaul was confronted by Yahusha in Person on his way to Damascus. Paul was gifted with skills and mentored by Gamilial. Gamalial was the grandson of the noble Turah teacher Hillel.
Paul was able to speak to anyone who would listen, and was not intimidated in the least by any lawyers, judges, sophists, governors or kings.
One of my favorite explanations of the **mission** of the Natsarim given to us by Yahusha is recorded in Acts 17. Paul was forcibly led-away by philosophers who overheard him teaching about a man resurrecting from the dead.
They took him to the **city council** of Athens. Paul respectfully answered their questions, and spoke eloquently of the true Creator. The city rulers were judges called the Areopagus, a council dating back 500 years before his lifetime. The ruling council members were called **areopagites**, and would have been ultimately responsible for any outside threats to the community's social, religious, economic, or well-being. They were compelled to do so by a legal code, or constitution. Paul's words were new to them, **especially his report of a man that had *risen from the dead***.
Let's re-read how Paul addressed these nobles of the Areopagus. The court who listened to Paul was a body of as many as 400 nobles who met together to preserve the cultural norms of the Athenian city- state. Enemies of the city-state were evaluated by their council according to a **law code** put into effect many centuries before them by their most renowned areopagite, **Solon.** (630-560 BCE) As you read Acts 17 carefully, try to put yourself in that time and place, and how Paul gives the *warning of the Natsarim* to the men of the council of Athens with a precision rarely heard today.
The idols of the Athenians were all around the city, yet Paul spoke with boldness to them all (the areopagites) about their ignorance concerning the coming Day of Yahuah to draw them out of their *worthless mythologies*. Keep in mind that Acts 17 was written at least 30+ years after Yahusha rose from the dead, which gave proof to all men that He would judge all men at His coming.

PAUL AT THE AREOPAGUS
ACTS 17:15-34 "And those who arranged for Paul brought him to Athens. And receiving a command for Sila and Timothy to join him

as soon as possible, they departed. But while Paul was waiting for them at Athens, his heart was stirred up within him when he saw that the city was wantonly idolatrous.

Therefore, indeed, he was reasoning in the assembly with the Yahudim and with the gentile worshippers, and in the market-place daily with those who met there. And some of the Epicurean and Stoic philosophers encountered him. And some were saying, 'What does this babbler wish to say?'

Others said, 'He seems to be a proclaimer of strange mighty ones' because he brought them the besorah:

Yahusha and the resurrection!

So they **laid hold of him** and brought him to the **Areopagus**, saying, 'Are we able to know what this fresh teaching is of which you speak? For you are bringing some strange things to our ears. We wish, then, to know what these things mean.'

For all the Athenians and the strangers living there spent their leisure time in doing nothing but to speak or to hear what is current. And having stood in the midst of the Areopagus Paul said, 'Men of Athens, I see that you are very pious in every way. For passing through and observing the **objects** of your worship, I even found an altar with this inscription:

TO THE UNKNOWN MIGHTY ONE

Not knowing then whom you worship, I make Him known to you: Yahuah, Who made the world and all that is in it, this One being Master of heaven and arets, does not dwell in dwellings made with hands. Nor is He served with men's hands – as if needing any – Himself giving to all life, and breath, and all else. And He has made from one blood every nation of men to dwell on all the face of the arets, having established beforehand the times and the boundaries of their dwelling, to seek the Master, if at least they would reach out for Him and find Him, though He is not far from each one of us. For in Him we live and move and are, as also some of your own poets have said, 'For we are also His offspring.' Now then, since we are the offspring of Alahim, we should not think that Alahim is like gold or silver or stone, an image made by the skill and thought of man. Truly, then, having overlooked these times of ignorance, Alahim now commands all men everywhere to repent, because He has set a yom on which He is going to **judge** the world in uprightness by a Man whom He has appointed, **having given proof of this to all by**

raising Him from the dead.' And hearing of the resurrection of the dead, some indeed mocked, while others said, 'We shall hear you again concerning this.' And so Paul went out from among them. But some men joined him and believed, among them Dionusios the areopagite, and an ashah named Damaris, and others with them." - Acts 17:15-34

THE AREOPAGITES WERE 400 JUDGES
PAUL TOLD THEM THE NAME OF THEIR JUDGE

As Paul spoke, **hundreds** of judges sat listening to him explain how silly it was to pray to idols made by men. These men were former **archons** who served as officers in government, and were highly educated nobles. Paul spoke the warning message of the Natsarim. The **Council of Areopagus** was in session, and Paul was standing in front of probably the full council of 400 men.

At the time Paul spoke to the council, their ethical guide was the **Solonian Constitution**, or the *code of Solon*.

Acts 17 is Luke's record of an event that brought the **warning message of the Natsarim into full view of the most *erudite** men of Paul's time.**

All people on Earth need to re-read the warning message at Acts 17 now, because the day Paul spoke of is about to arrive.
*CLEVER, INFORMED

Paul's words to Timothy (2 Tim. 4:1-6) tell us how **sound doctrine** would be abandoned, and the teachers are the cause for it. They have taught against obedience, and withheld the Name.

PASTORS: *YOU HAVE A CHOICE*

You can keep teaching the traditions of your fathers, or turn back to truth. You have been doing all the things the Pharisees and lawyers did; you control doctrines, restraining all who desire to live by Yahuah's Word.

You have wandered *far* from sound doctrines and invented trigger-words like *Judaizer* and *legalism*. Yahusha has nothing in common with Sunday, Easter, Christmas, birthdays, or making wishes to genies and blowing out candles. Find out what these used to be before they were *adopted* by Christianity.

The traditions of the world are familiar to everyone, glued to each family unit, and are unchallenged by pastors who fear they will lose their place if they expose them.

"Come out of her, My people!"
It's about to get very serious.

Yahusha quoted YashaYahu (Isaiah):

"And Yahuah says, 'Because this people has drawn near with its mouth, and with its lips they have esteemed Me, and it has kept its heart far from Me, and their fear of Me has become a command of men that is taught. Therefore, see, I am again doing a marvelous work among this people, a marvelous work and a wonder. And the wisdom of their wise men shall perish, and the understanding of their clever men shall be hidden."
YashaYahu 29:13-14 - see also Mt. 15:8

IF THEY DON'T KNOW, HOW WILL THEY HEAR UNLESS SOMEONE IS SENT TO SPEAK TO THEM?
Acts 17 - 2 Timothy 4:1-6 - Malaki 4:1-6

The Blood Of Animals vs. The Blood Of The Lamb
Life is in the blood. To offer the life of an animal's blood was the schoolmaster, showing the seriousness of sin, and pointed to the perfect offering that redeems all who trust in Yahusha. The former covered temporarily; the latter redeems completely. Works are different than works. It all depends on what the word 'works' is referring to. Works (animal blood) of the law are different than works of obedience. Obeying is better than offerings every time. Due to false ideas promoted by men and their own imaginations, the whole world is more confused than ever. Natsarim are tearing down strongholds, which are false ideas inherited from the past.

The Truth will set you free from these if you allow Yahusha to give you His perspective, and learn to walk as He walked. Let's begin with two Scriptures that always seem to get twisted by teachers.

Does Ephesians 2:8–9 Conflict With James 2:20?
The phrase 'belief without works is dead' at Yaqub / James 2:20 only seems in conflict with Ephesians 2:8–9. When we understand Paul is referring to the *former covenant using the works of animal blood offered by an obsolete priesthood*, we see no conflict. Yaqub is referring to *obeying the Ten Commandments, and showing our core beliefs expressed in our outward behavior.* This is also what he meant by saying **"be doers of the Word, not hearers only."** (See Yaqub 1:22–25)

The misunderstanding is the fault of our teachers, just as Paul told Timothy at 2 Timothy 4:2–4. Not holding to sound teaching, they surrounded themselves with teachers tickling their ears, and turned aside to myths.

Obeying is better than slaughtering. We show our belief by obedience, doing the Word, and not hearers only. Yahusha compels us to see as He does. Is there any Scripture anyone can quote that mentions shatan teaching legalism? Legalism is a made-up term invented to keep people away from doing what is pleasing to Yahusha. Shatan hates us to obey Yahuah's Turah.
Paul says we must not continue sinning so that favor may abound (Romans 6), but at our immersion* we no longer are slaves to sin. Our belief in Yahusha's blood has overcome the world, and we are no longer under the authority of the evil one, but under the protection of Yahusha our Redeemer. Obedience was, is, and always will be the evidence of the one we serve.
We are not free TO sin, but free FROM sin.
*(our pledge to **obey**, calling on Yahusha for forgiveness of our sins)

Dancing With The Devil
For illustration, let's lump all those who use **titles** under one category: *gurus*.
Gurus lure people with all kinds of promises of enlightenment and fulfillment. They teach against obeying the Commandments, which Ecclesiastes 12:13-14 confirms for us as critically important, and they are easy to obey. Gurus say the Ten Commandments are too difficult, and cannot be obeyed. Some have said they are a curse. But the curse was the law that was added due to transgressions, not the Turah of Yahuah, His instructions that teach love, making us wise. Why do people listen to gurus, and not believe the Word of Yahuah? Belief without obedience is dead, and unperfected. Hebrews 11 and Yaqub 2:14-26 explains this very well.
It is because the gurus promote the strong delusion, sent to those who would not receive a love for the Truth, which is Yahuah's Word. The secret is with those who fear Yahuah, and He makes His Covenant known to them (Ps. 25:14). The gurus are leading the conga line, and all the world is dancing on the brink of oblivion because they are following the king of Babel, Satan. The **first**

Natsarim followed Yahusha; the **last Natsarim** are here now, crying out on the hills of Afraim (YirmeYahu 31:6).

What Was The Old Covenant?
The old covenant was hand-written on a sefer (scroll) and placed beside the ark (Dt. 31:26). It is now obsolete, only offering animal blood as directed through the old priesthood (Hebrews 8:13).
This process was replaced by the renewed Covenant through Yahusha's one-time offering His Own blood, providing for the complete redemption of all mankind. Our belief in His blood as our complete atoning offering is expressed to Him by calling on His Name as our Deliverer as we are immersed in water, pledging our whole life to Him as an obedient servant. He then imparts His life in us to receive a love for the Truth (His Word). He lives in us, and we no longer live. From this beginning point, we are begotten from above, sealed for the day of the redemption of our bodies. It is our pledge of marriage to Him, and He cleans us from the inside so the outward behavior will also be clean. He writes a love for His Covenant on our hearts (thinking processes).
The Ten Commandments are eternal, and is the Covenant of marriage between Yahuah and all those He calls to become His bride. It was written in the stone tablets inside the ark, and Yahusha has written a love for these Ten Words on the tablets of our hearts. The Circus has deceived billions up until now, the Truth will set you free. Come out of Babel, and stop being deceived by that old harlot.
www.fossilizedcustoms.com/ten.html

The Temple Mount Faithful
Their desire is to re-start the animal sacrifices for sin.
The formal ending of the animal blood requirement was when Yahusha shed His blood, and He described it for us the night before at the supper when He lifted the cup. They didn't get it right away either. He has redeemed us by His blood *completely*. Hebrews (Eberim) speaks of the change in the priesthood, and its "growing old" and about to disappear. Paul was using the format of the Nazir oath to influence his own who were under Turah when others urged him to take the oath while the Temple was standing, but he was *interrupted* just as he was in the midst of it, being arrested by men accusing him of speaking against Turah and the Temple. His accusers were lying because they knew he was

serious a threat, having excelled above all others of his age in the traditions of the fathers. The Temple Mount Faithful have not thought the whole arrangement through to its logical conclusion. Even if every item and person involved in re-starting the animal sacrifices comes together and the Muslims tear down their shivalingam standing where it should not be, where is the ark to place in the set-apart place? Oopsy, Yahuah has it, it appeared in the heavens (Rev. 11:19) at the seventh trump, and the nations were enraged. How many animals would it take to be offered for one single act of transgression? Think about this, and reason will tell you there is no comparison - the perfect offering is made.
Yahuah has provided **Himself** as the Lamb. Animal blood delivers no one, but was only a schoolmaster pointing to the True Lamb.

Scripture calls itself the **Scripture of Truth** (kethab amath) at Danial 10:21. From it we learn we are delivered only by the blood of Yahusha, and *no longer is animal blood* used to temporarily cover our transgressions. Danial 12 tells us about the last days, when the wise will lead many to uprightness. The messenger Mikal tells Danial to seal the book until the time of the end, and many will roam, and knowledge will increase. We are now realizing those who teach us have put up of wall to keep us away from knowledge. During the *Dark Ages*, people were kept from learning anything except what the teaching authority wanted them to know.
The slightest deviations in behavior, or disrespect toward those of the 1st estate (clergy), were met with savage penalties. The age of Information has arrived, and we are able to communicate with one another, without many restrictions.
The linchpin of all human history is just ahead for mankind, when the Reign of Yahusha begins, and the reign of Babel (beast) falls. This change will come like a trap closing on a dumb animal. Ambassadors have been awakened to announce the coming of Yahusha to reign, and they are the Natsarim, the branches of His teachings, and those who guard the Commandments of Yahuah. The Second Exodus will be a world-wide event. An assembly of Natsarim will be clothed in light when Yahusha appears in the space above us, and every eye will see Him.
YashaYahu (Isaiah) describes it for us in the 24th and 25th chapters. Yahusha's arrival to reign will be announce that Yahuah is our Deliverer:

"He shall swallow up death forever, and Aduni Yahuah shall wipe away tears from all faces, and take away the reproach of His people from all the arets. For Yahuah has spoken. And it shall be said in that yom, 'See, this is our Alahim. We have waited for Him, and He saves us. This is Yahuah, we have waited for Him, let us be glad and rejoice in His deliverance.'"
YashaYahu 25:8-9 - BYNV

YirmeYahu (Jeremiah) tells us about it in these words:
"'Therefore see, the Yomim are coming,' says Yahuah, 'when it is no longer said, "Yahuah lives who brought up the children of Yisharal from the land of Mitsrim," but, "Yahuah lives who brought up the children of Yisharal from the land of the north and from all the lands where He had driven them." For I shall bring them back into their land I gave to their fathers.'"
YirmeYahu 16:14-15 - BYNV

The world has been unknowingly programmed to follow a cycle of fertility practices, re-invented to conceal their true origins.
The confusion about what we are to obey is being announced. What was whispered in the inner rooms is being shouted from the rooftops. The eternal Covenant (Ten Commandments) are to be taught and lived by. Most are kept from this knowledge by those who teach them. The Old Covenant was placed *beside* the ark, written by hand on a **scroll** (Dt. 31:26, Hebrews 8:13). The old priesthood has grown *obsolete*, and by Yahusha's indwelling we have received a love for the Truth, His living Word circumcising our hearts to love the Ten Commandments. Men have invented *sacraments*, as well as a priesthood to dispense them, returning to *ceremonies*. They all pretend together, resulting in a form of mass-hypnosis. The book **Strong Delusion** will explain how this happened over time.
All who call on the Name of Yahusha will be delivered.
YAHU+SHA means *I am your* + the suffix, *deliverer*.

In the **Scripture of Truth** you can find references to a Vine, a Root, and those abiding in the Root called the branches.
At Yahukanon (John) 15:5 we see these important references to the Natsarim: "I am the Vine (GAFEN), and you are the branches (NATSARIM)." At Acts 24:5, Paul is accused of being a ringleader of the **"sect of the Natsarim"** by Tertullus, a hired sophist sent by the High Priest.

Today, the Yahudim in Yerushalum call those who believe in the Mashiak **NOTSRIM.** We are prophesied to appear on the hills (mountains, the nations) of Afraim in the extreme last days **to announce the coming reign of Yahusha** (see YirmeYahu 31:6). The word *watchmen* is the Hebrew word Natsarim, the branches.

NATSARIM ARE VERY REAL

We were prophesied to appear at YirmeYahu 31:6, and Revelation 12:17 explains we are the *first-fruits,* enraging the dragon because we obey the Commandments of Alahim and hold the Testimony of Yahusha. Christianity was born at Alexandria, Egypt, and reinforced by the authority of Rome beginning at Nicaea in 325 CE.

The Natsarim were based at Antioch just prior to the destruction of the Temple, and had to hide themselves from the Christian Magisterium for over 1000 years. We were forced to dwell in the hills and valleys, and called Passagans, Albigensians, Waldenses, and Huguenots. We are proclaiming the Name of Yahusha around the world as His envoys.

The Deliverer is **Yahusha**, not **Jesus**. This is an identity theft the Natsarim are here to correct.

There is only one Name by which we are to be delivered, and it is Hebrew: **Yahusha** (see Acts 4:12), not Greek, English, or Latin.
The dragon is enraged by us, and we are the first-fruits who guard the Commandments of Yahuah and hold to the testimony of Yahusha (see Rev. 12:17).

Do You Love All Ten Commandments Yet?

Would you like to *love* the Commandments? There is only one way to receive a love for them; Yahusha must circumcize your heart (mind, thinking patterns) with His perspective of you and everything around you. You have to take on His perspective of the kosmos. Pursue His zone of purpose, the reason for which you were created, with all your strength.

My own discovery of His purpose for creating me was an awakening. When we awaken, the delusions we were involved in from our childhood clear away like a fog dispersing. We have to turn around, and stop resisting the Creator's will, and just do it. It is never about what *we* desire, but rather to learn to cooperate with the Creator and His purpose. Doing things His way always works for the good of everyone. We were designed to perform (live in, abide in) the Commandments. They are easy, perfect, and everlasting (See Psalm 119, Ecclesiastes 12:13-14). Receive a love of the Truth, or be sent a strong delusion to believe the lie of the serpent. If we abide in the Truth, we are truly His talmidim, and we will know the Truth, and the Truth will set us free. Disobedience will always lead astray.

Who Are Natsarim?
We are the Bride, the Higher Calling, the First-fruits, the Treasured Possession. We have been awakened to announce the coming of Yahusha, and prepared the remnant to bring forth to Him a purified bride without wrinkled, dirty garments.

PAUL WAS A RINGLEADER OF THE SECT IN HIS DAY
You will be shocked to see this in any translation at **Acts 24:5**:
"For having found this man a plague, who stirs up dissension among all the Yahudim throughout the world, and a ringleader of the sect of the NATSARIM . . ."

Natsarim is a Hebrew word meaning *branches*. It also means *watchmen*.
It is found in the Hebrew text at YirmeYahu 31:6, the chapter where the renewal of the Covenant is found. We are branches of Yahusha's teaching authority, abiding in His Word, or yoke (teachings).
We are not only branches of His teachings, but also guardians (watchmen) over His WORD, and His NAME. Natsarim is translated *watchmen* at YirmeYahu 31:6.
Please try to read this passage now, and again after you read this eBook.

Also read Psalm 80 which describes our work in the end times.
After the destruction of the Temple in 70 CE by Titus, two groups emerged: the **PHARISEES** (aka Prushim, or *separate ones*) and the **NATSARIM**. The **Karaites** split-off from the Prushim in the 8th century CE (founder: Anan, 767 CE), looking at crescents. Pharisees teach the *traditions of the fathers* and Turah. They have been especially unkind to Natsarim, who behave very closely as for the Turah, but because we ignore their "teaching authority" we are perceived to be a threat to that authority. They are the exalted ones, or rabbis, but we have only One Who is our Rabbi, Yahusha. We are under only His teachings (yoke).

The *Shemoneh Esrei* (prayer #18) recited each Shabath among those Yahudim who have not yet acknowledged Yahusha is a curse on the Natsarim. They refer to us as the *minim*.

We love those who curse us, and do good to those who hate us. If they treated our Leader Yahusha as they did, we can expect no different treatment. He was perceived to be a threat to their teaching authority, so they eventually managed to have Him brought up on charges of blasphemy. That may happen to us at any time, because we proclaim the Name of Yahuah, as did Yahusha. They stoned Stephen for saying the Name in their Sanhedrin.

SCROLL OF REMEMBRANCE
Scripture provides us with words that identify the **Natsarim**.
You'll find them called the **bride**, **first-fruits**, **wise managers**, a **treasured possession**, and a **higher-calling** - all of these are referring to them because they will be in the first resurrection at Yahusha's coming, rather than at the end of the Millennium.

Yahuah consistently contrasts the difference between those who **serve** Him from those who **do not serve** Him.

Most people are aware of the **Scroll of Life** mentioned in Scripture, but there is another scroll that contains the names of Yahuah's *"treasured possession."*

"Then shall those who fear Yahuah shall speak to one another, and Yahuah will listen and hear, and a *Scroll of Remembrance* be written before Him of those who fear Yahuah, and *those who think upon His Name.*
'And they shall be Mine,' said Yahuah Tsabaoth, 'on the day that

I prepare a *treasured possession*. And I shall spare them as a man spares his own son who serves Him. Then you shall again see the difference between the righteous and the wrong, between one who serves Alahim and one who does not serve Him.'" - Malaki 3:16-18

The **Name** (Yahuah) and the **Word** (His Commandments) are **above all** (Ps 138:2).

How can they **call** unless someone is sent to **speak** to them? This is written for a generation to be born that they might call on the Name of Yahuah (Ps. 102:18). All Scripture is **written** down as the very words of Yahuah, Mosheh being the first person inspired to use the Name *Yahusha* for his servant Husha. Yahuah give us the desires of our hearts to accomplish His purposes, and we are all like a huge orchestra following His cues for a beautiful sound to come out of our lips. He inhabits our praises to His Name.

Paul co-relates the sounds of our lips to musical instruments: *"But now, brothers, if I come to you speaking with tongues, what shall I profit you unless I speak to you, either by revelation, or by knowledge, or by prophesying, or by teaching? Nevertheless, lifeless instruments making a sound, whether flute or harp, if they do not make a distinction in the sound, how shall it be known what is played on the flute or on the harp? For indeed, if the trumpet makes an indistinct sound, who shall prepare himself for battle? So also you, if you do not give speech by the tongue that is clear, how shall it be known what is spoken? For you shall be speaking into the air. There are, undoubtedly, so many kinds of sounds in the world, and none of them is without comprehensible sound."* - 1 Korinthians 14:6-10 *BYNV*

In the vast majority of translations, the Name was not used at all, but replaced with encryptions like **IHS**, **IESV**, **IC-XC**, and other words meaning *LORD*. Aduni, Kyrios, Dominus, and LORD are translations from the Hebrew word BEL (beth-ayin-lamed, aka: Baal)

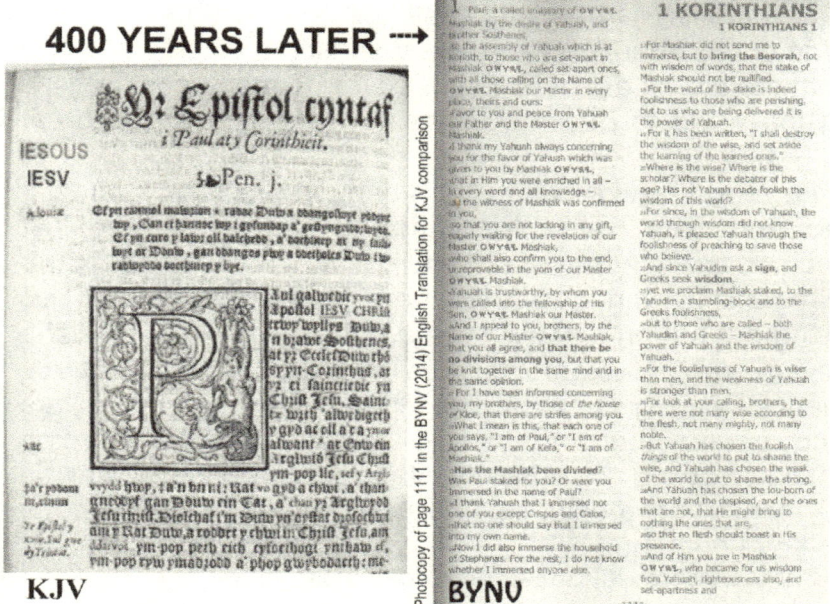

TEACHING AUTHORITY

The **Natsarim** have never recognized any teaching authority but one: **Yahusha**.

The Sanhedrin asked Yahusha what **teaching authority** had given Him permission to teach (Mt. 21:23). Before the destruction of the Temple at Yerushalayim, the Natsarim had their base of operations at Antioch (see Acts 11, 14, 15, & 18). Over the next several centuries, a false teaching authority was growing in power at Alexandria, Egypt. After the destruction of the Yerushalayim Temple in 70, the Natsarim dispersed into every direction. Their persecutors mentioned them occasionally as being heretics, because they **obeyed the Commandments** and ignored the teaching authority of the circus fathers. To them, the Natsarim seemed no different than the Yahudim in their practices, except they believed in Yahusha.

Becoming Prey To Men's Philosophies?

Traditions of men have replaced the teachings of Yahusha, and His example of living with ancient pagan fertility festivals. They are cloaked among family activities, such as blowing out candles and making wishes, and singing a spell to the celebrant. Raising toasts (drink offerings), hanging mistletoe and wreaths, cutting ribbons at grand openings, and every seasonal display you can think of at the stores are concealing their true meanings: fertility, causing the world to become drunk from the cup of the great mother, Babel.

When you read the word *Jesus*, it stands in place of Yahusha, His true and only Name. **Nicolaitanes** are roaring against obedience. Lawlessness is still increasing because of them. Kolossians 2:8-10 warns us of teachers' **philosophies** (traditions) dominating our patterns of living, and not the example Yahusha has given us. Sacraments, divination (consulting spirits), necromancy (praying to the dead), repetitive prayers, pillars (steeples), circumambulating around objects, Sunday morning assembling, bowing or kissing statues, believing water is blessed, consulting mediums, and much more are all serious idolatry. Love one another.

www.fossilizedcustoms.com/idolatry.html

Discern How You Hear Teachers Saying

If someone is actively teaching you to ignore any one of the Ten Commandments, it is evident they do not know what they are talking about, and they need help. They profess knowing Yahusha, but they deny Him by their actions (Titus 1:16).

"Now the goal of this command is love from a clean heart, from a good conscience and a sincere belief, which some, having missed the goal, turned aside to senseless talk, wishing to be teachers of Turah, understanding neither what they say nor concerning what they strongly affirm."
1 Timothy 1:5-7 BYNV

What Is EISEGESIS?

Hunting-down verses to *proof-text an idea or practice* is called *eisegesis*, and illustrates how easy it is to deceive people. They are not exposed to the whole context, but only parts of verses. Consider Acts 20 where Luke writes about Paul being in a rush to get to Yerushalom for the festival of Shabuoth (v. 16). Paul stopped in several places like Troas along the way: Acts 20:6 tells us,

"But we sailed from Philippi after the Festival of Unleavened Bread, and five days later joined the others at Troas, where we stayed seven days. Paul was preparing to depart from Troas

after staying there 7 days, so after the Sun had set on the 7th day, there was a gathering in an upper room "on the *first* of the Shabaths"
- *the first Shabath in the count to Shabuoth*, which is always the morrow after the 7th Shabath. There were many lamps in the upper room where they were listening to Paul speak. It was night, and Paul spoke until midnight. This is not teaching anyone to observe the rising Sun deity's steeple meetings, but clearly twisted by men inventing their own methods of worship.

What Was The Schoolmaster?
Read Malaki 4:1-6, the Turah (instruction of Mushah) is to be obeyed, otherwise Yahuah will destroy the entire Earth.
Teachers are confused, and mix the Turah inside the ark (now written on our hearts) with the Turah outside the ark (animal blood, the **schoolmaster** leading us to Yahusha's one-time offering of His own blood). They want be teachers, but they do not submit to the Truth (Yahuah's Word). They cast His Words behind them, yet claim to be teachers of His Word.
"To the wicked He says, 'What gives you the right to recite My statutes and to take My Covenant on your lips? For you hate My Turah and cast My Words behind you?'" - Ps. 50:15-17

I love Yahusha and obey His Commandments willingly, as He has written them on my heart. Satan wants all men to be *disobedient*, and teaches them to disobey through messengers masquerading as teachers of righteousness. If anyone refuses to receive a love of the Truth, Yahuah sends them a **strong delusion** to believe the lie. The mind of the flesh is unwilling to obey, nor can it; but the Mind of the Spirit (Mashiak in you) enables you to obey, because He gives us the *same viewpoint of sin that He has*. Those who do not know Him do not obey, nor can they; neither do they belong to Him.
It's easy to obey His Commandments, just as He said at 1Yn 5:2-4. This is how we know that we know Him (1 Yahukanon 2:3): if we guard His Commandments. The question is, do you love Him enough to obey Him? I hope the answer will be YES! Be restored to favor by repenting of sin, and Ecclesiates 12:13-14 will make sense.

RamaBamahDingDong! (Bells / gongs origins: Hinduism)
A familiar symbol of Babel rises high on the horizon of every city

and town on Earth: **steeples**.
I asked a pastor about what the steeple on his building signified, without any traditional guile (deceit, duplicity). The pastors all know what they are, but they will all say,
"I know, but without the spire, how will anyone know it's a church?"
Pastors of all denominations know what will happen to them if they confute the least of men's traditions, all inherited from Babel.
They fear the dragon more than Yahusha.
Time is short, and the urgency for sharing the Truth must be taken directly to the source of all the teaching errors: pastors. They are skilled at defending lies.
Where in the Scriptures of Truth are we told to erect a steeple, or meet with others to give our money to a pastor every week in a specialized building to support their lies? Each of these buildings is in close proximity to another building with similar design, holding a different mix of ideas (denomination) but all claiming to teach 100% Truth. Each building is used once or twice a week for one purpose: to support the brand of intoxicating lies their itching ears want to hear. (2Timothy 4:3-4)
Steeples are widely-approved identity marks among the SDA's, Mormons, Baptists, Amish, Baptists, Mennonites, Charismatic / Pentecostals, Eastern Orthodox, Roman & Anglican Catholics, Presbyterians, non-denominational Christians, Scientology, Jehovah Witnesses, and so many other groups, yet they have all been very successful because people do not test what is taught.
"For such are false emissaries, deceptive workers, masquerading as emissaries of Mashiak. And no wonder! For shatan himself masquerades as a messenger of light! It is not surprising, then, if his servants also masquerade as servants of uprightness, whose end shall be according to their works!" 2 Korinthians 11:13-15

To erect high places is forbidden. A common Hebrew term for a high place is BAMAH.
Yahusha will certainly rama-bamah some ding-dongs when He returns. Natsarim are here to spread the real message so more people will come out of the *reign of Babel*, be *restored to favor*, and *love one another*, no matter what.

www.fossilizedcustoms.com/steeplepeople.html

NATSARIM ARE VERY REAL

We were prophesied to appear at YirmeYahu 31:6, and Revelation 12:17 explains we are the first-fruits, enraging the dragon because we obey the Commandments of Alahim and hold the Testimony of Yahusha. Christianity was born at Alexandria, Egypt, and reinforced by the authority of Rome beginning at Nicaea in 325 CE. The Natsarim were based at Antioch just prior to the destruction of the Temple, and had to hide themselves from the Christian Magisterium for over 1000 years. We were forced to dwell in the hills and valleys, and called Passagans, Albigensians, Waldenses, and Huguenots. We are proclaiming the Name of Yahusha around the world as His envoys. A Catholic website mentioned this author's name, and I attempted to answer their questions about the Natsarim, but was blocked permanently. I saved the discourse we had up to that point:

CATHOLIC FORUM TOPIC: NATSARIM
A BRIEF CONVERSATION BETWEEN A JESUIT AND A NATSARI

Because my name (Lew White) came up on a Catholic forum,
I registered to respond to several questions being asked about what they referred to as *"the cult of the Natsarim."*
This is the entire, but brief, interaction I had with the Jesuits. You will find their final response very interesting.

Catholic forum topic: NATSARIM
The original post on the forum asked the question:

Jesuit question to the forum:

Has anyone heard of the cult of the Natsarim? What are it's core beliefs and how does it relate to Jewish and Christian religion??

(This is my original reply to the question, because my name was mentioned in the forum as being in a cult, the Natsarim):

My reply:
The term **NATSARIM** is used to describe the original followers of Yahusha of Natsarith at Acts 24:5. The term *Christianos* is found 3 times in the Greek, but the term was, in that time, a Greek term of scorn, used in a list of other scornful labels at 1 Peter 5:8.
The Hebrew/Yisharali followers of Yahusha did not call themselves by a **Greek** term, but were at first **called** *Christianos* at Antioch, according to Acts 11:26. If you look up the term **cretin** you will find it is traced back to the original Greek, **Christianos** a scornful term used in that time to describe a simpleton, or an idiot. The term later was adopted by those at *Alexandria*, and propelled by the headmasters of the Catechetical School of Alexandria.

For every weird accusation there is a logical, truthful answer; my reputation has been commonly smeared, but so was the "cult" called Natsarim in the days of the first followers - Acts 28:22:

"And we think it right to hear from you what you think, for indeed, concerning this sect, we know that it is spoken against everywhere." (a sect is a subset or variation from a larger group or culture, hopefully motivated to remove erroneous teachings)

Jesuit reply:
But am I to understand you are yet another group of Judaisers?

My reply:
Catholics refer to those who rest on the Sabbath by the term ***Judaizers***. *Heresy* is the strongest accusation one group will accuse another one of. Strong (and deadly) disputes arise between groups who share similar, but not identical beliefs. Sunni and Shia are similar, but not identical, and so each group considers the other heretics.
Since the 12th century, the **Natsarim** (aka Huguenots, Waldensians, Pasagians, Cathars, Albigenses, Ebionites) kept the Commandments as written (including the true Sabbath, not Sun-day), and were brutally

attacked by German, French, and Bohemian armies for centuries, long before the *Reformation*.

The WIKIPEDIA ENCYCLOPEDIA states:
"The Roman Catholic Church declared them heretics — stating the group's principal error was **'contempt for ecclesiastical power'**. The ***Waldensians*** were also accused by the Catholic Church of teaching 'innumerable errors'."

JUDAIZER is the label often used today for those who obey Turah, however at Galatians 2:14 it specifically was over adult male circumcision - Paul confronted Peter over this point, and it was finally decided on as recorded at Acts 15, with Yahusha's brother James (Yaqub, aka Jacob) presiding over the Natsarim assembly (he was the Nasi, or president of the Natsarim). If we obey the true Sabbath, and teach love, obedience to Turah, we are accused of being Judaizers, and thus heretics. The fruit of the tree is the way you determine the kind of tree it is. We Natsarim teach love, which is the outcome of guarding the Commandments. The bad fruit, centuries of extermination, including before the Inquisition existed, must be placed in another divisional camp, which will be judged by Yahusha, not me or any other Natsari.

We are to love, teach, and obey; not judge.

We are labeled heretics because we love the Commandments, and shun the Nicolaitane *"ecclesiastical powers."* We still love our enemies, and don't kill them. We hold no power, nor pursue it. Yahusha is our Head, we are His body. The fruit identifies the tree it hangs on.

Jesuit reply:
Lew, You did not answer my question. **You just lost credibility and earned a report to the forum masters**. I believe that you are proselytizing ...You are preaching.

My reply:
I'm not preaching, I'm addressing the question. Specifically, the question was: ***are we a sect of Judaizers?*** The *context* is often misunderstood, since a Judaizer referenced from Galatians 2:14 pertains to circumcision, which is the book Paul wrote addressing the topic of circumcision. Catholicism condemns those who **rest on the Sabbath** as Judaizers, and they even refer to the Sabbath in their decision from the Council of Laodicea in 365 in 59 laws, Canon #29:

"Christians must not Judaize by resting on the Sabbath, but must work on that day, rather honoring the Lord's Day; and if they can, resting then as Christians. But if any shall be found to be Judaizers, let them be anathema from Christ."

One would have to concede that Yahusha and all His followers would be anathema according to this dogma. The law even makes reference to *"the Sabbath,"* so they acknowledge it is a **real day of each week**. The council orders that **work be done on the Sabbath**. Who would teach this to be pleasing to Yahuah?
Romans 6:16 tells us the one we obey is the one we serve.
You did not know this?

Jesuit reply:
Do you regard the Natsarim as the true Messianic Judaism and do you strictly follow Turah Law?

My reply:
There is no such thing as *Messianic Judaism*. This term was invented to describe those who may be of the tribe of Yahudah, but also practice rabbinical Judaism, based on Talmud as well as Turah, began by a rabbi - or exalted one - named Akiba, 2nd century. Rab is a Hebrew root meaning *chief*, as in *Rabshakeh*, *chief cup-bearer*.
The true faith of the followers of Yahusha involves belief in His atonement (by His blood sprinkling our hearts, or inner spirits), **and walking in the way He walked; in Turah.** We are obliged to go, teach all nations what *we* were commanded to obey, and that is easily found at Ex. 20, Lev. 11, and Lev. 23. It's not difficult in the least, and in fact a very light *yoke* (teaching). There's only one rabbi, Yahusha.
BTW, there's no such thing as a *Palestinian* either.
The word *Palestine* is based on the term *Philistine*, and is a Latinization. Philistines no longer exist as a people anywhere.
Natsarim are very real however.

Jesuit reply:
So you reject the Oral Law (Talmud) as being transmitted by G-d together with the Written Law (Turah)? That would be similar to Karaite Judaism. Do you then consider the Natsarim the only true Christians, apart from using the term itself?

My reply:

There is no such thing as an *oral law*. As for our similarities with Karaites, the TaNaK is the basis of the revelation of Truth; but unlike them we also embrace the writings of the Brith Chadasha (referred to as the "New Testament" by Christianity). We overcome **strongholds** (mental fortresses of errant beliefs) by the indwelling of the Spirit of Yahusha Who guides us into Truth and discernment.

He gives His Spirit to those who obey Him (Acts 5:32).

We are not a *religion*. We are guardians of the **Name** (Yahuah) and His **Word** (Turah), which He has exalted above all (see Ps. 25:14, Ps. 138:2).

This forum asked the question, **what are the 'core beliefs' of the Natsarim?** - you're communicating with one of the Natsarim now.

Jesuit reply:

Thank you for your informative responses. One more question: do you believe in the divinity of Jesus? I assume you don't believe in the Trinity; am I correct?

My reply:

Yahusha is Yahuah, as He revealed to Philip (Yn 14:9). **"Have I been with you so long, and you have not known me Phillip? He who has seen Me, has seen the Father . . ."** Sorry, but there's no "trinity" revealed as a teaching in Scripture. It came along much later as a part of the creed developed pertaining to "baptism" (immersion in water, our pledge of a good conscience toward Yahuah, and our commitment/marriage/joining to Him). The Spirit is Yahuah, but since Yahuah is the **same Person** as Yahusha, there is but ONE Person, not three -- unless you can produce a text of Scripture that actually teaches there are *three persons*.

(Acts 20:28 says the Ruach ha Qodesh purchased the assembly "with His Own blood.")

We are keen to discern between "exegesis" and "eisegesis."

Our *wineskins* are new, and only accept the teaching authority of Yahusha. Old wine (men's traditions) will not remain where the "new wine" (Yahusha's Word/teachings) have been accepted.

The Light drives away the darkness, overcoming it completely. If Yahuah were truly **3 persons**, He would have surely told us.

Most Pagan religions involved 3 (**Baal Shalishi** - "3 LORD"); all derive from Babel: **Nimrod, Tammuz, & Semiramis.**

BAAL is Hebrew for "LORD," so we don't substitute His Name for "LORD" either. These are just some details that may be interesting, I'm not intending to upset anyone.

Jesuit reply:
Your account has been locked for the following reason:
Trolling, agenda posting
This change will be lifted: Never
The site also removed each posting where they conversed with me, and all my responses.
This is the webpage where I have preserved this conversation:
http://www.fossilizedcustoms.com/catholicforum.html

Where Is The Menorah?

Imagine how horrifying it must have been on the 9th of Av in the year 70 CE for the inhabitants of Yerushalom. The 9th day of the month of Av recalls the day the Temple of Yahuah was destroyed, first by Nebuchanezzar, and a second time on the same date by Titus. Two arches and a Colosseum were built at Rome with the booty they carried away. The golden menorah is still somewhere, hidden away in Rome. Inside the arch of Titus, you can still see how excited the Romans were to have such a prize, yet their faces show how they sense something ominous will happen for having done this to Yahuah's people.

34

Yahusha has allowed the removal of our menorah, and driven us into the nations, but He will restore everything His enemies have taken; He's the Possessor of Heaven and Earth.
www.Torahzone.net/Fossilized-Customs-12th-Edition.html

Yahuah Is Our Alahim; Yahuah Is One

Dt. 6:4 and Yaqub 2:19 tell us there is one Alahim, and even the demons believe and shudder. Philip did not quite understand Who Yahusha is, but if we ask Him, He will tell us. Yahukanon 14:6-10 puts it right out there for us, and there can be only One to serve:

"Yahusha said to him, 'I am the Way, and the Truth, and the Life. No one comes to the Father except through Me. If you had known Me, you would have known My Father too. From now on you know Him, and have seen.' Philip said to Him, 'Aduni, show us the Father, and it is enough for us.' Yahusha said to him, 'Have I been with you so long, and you have not known Me, Philip? He who has seen Me has seen the Father, and how do you say, "Show us the Father?" Do you not believe that I am in the Father, and the Father is in Me?"'

MatithYahu 11:27 explains how only Yahusha can reveal Himself to a person:

"All have been handed over to Me by My Father, and no one knows the Son except the Father. Nor does anyone know the Father except the Son, and he to whom the Son wishes to reveal Him."

Yahusha claimed **He** is Al Shaddai at Rev. 1:8. This is a very penetrating question, **"Who do you say that I am?"** If we believe what Yahusha says, and not the teachers building fences around the Truth, we are truly His talmidim.

Be like a Berean. The Name of Yahusha is offensive to most because it reveals that someone has lied to them. The name most of the world thinks is the correct name for our Creator, Who is also our Redeemer, is very recent in origin. The One that shed His blood to redeem us all deserves to receive praise, not an invented word less than 500 years old. Google: YAHUSHA. Our teachers are leading us **away** from the Name, and teaching disobedience. Yahusha told us the last days would be severe, and at Mt. 24:20 told us to pray our flight not be on a Shabath, so we have fallen very far from the path. All who call upon the Name will be delivered.

He also told Yahukanon to write to an assembly at Ephesus to repent, and do the first works, or He will remove their menorah. Yahusha's Name identifies Him. A surprisingly large number of people fall for the idea of dividing the Scripture of Truth into **old** and **new**, a concept propagated in the 2nd century by Marcion.
In Marcion's case, the division was a complete separation from the old, while others do the opposite, and reject Yahusha and all the writings of the Natsarim.
There are many distractions and labels within the fractured belief groups, and each one tries to look and act differently than all the others. This is another reason the term *circus* fits so well to describe them all. **Unless Yahuah builds the house, the builders labor in vain** (Ps. 127:1).
Yahusha told us Scripture was referring to Him (Luke 24:44), and He identifies Himself to be Al Shaddai, and reveals He is the Alef-Tau, the Speaker inspiring the men of old that wrote all His words for us (Revelation 1:8-10).
We know it is only Yahusha's activity in any of us that we can do anything. As He said, without Him, we can do nothing. His pupils recognize one another very easily, and so do the ones He is working on! Love one another, no matter the personal cost.
www.Torahzone.net/Strong-Delusion-Book.html

Scripture Sources Matter, Traditions Don't

What have our teachers been using for their source of all Truth? The Sabbath is spoken of 9 times in the book of Acts. Luke wrote Acts in the early 60's (1st century).
Why do pastors tell everyone Shabath was not repeated in the "New Testament" (their terminology for the Natsarim Writings)?
One pastor claimed there is no record of any follower of Yahusha *(Whom he insists on calling "Jesus")* observing the 7th day of rest, or teaching it. At Acts 20:16, Paul was in a hurry to arrive at Yerushalom in time for Shabuoth (one of the annual appointed times!).
www.fossilizedcustoms.com/sabbath.html

What Is EISEGESIS?

Hunting-down verses to proof-text an idea or practice is called *eisegesis*, and illustrates how easy it is to deceive people.
They are not exposed to the whole context, but only parts of verses.

Consider Acts 20 where Luke writes about Paul being in a rush to get to Yerushalom for the festival of **Shabuoth** (v. 16).
Paul stopped in several places like Troas along the way. Acts 20:6: "But we sailed from Philippi after the Festival of Unleavened Bread, and five days later joined the others at Troas, where we stayed seven days. Paul was preparing to depart from Troas after staying there 7 days, so *after the Sun had set on the 7th day,* there was a gathering in an upper room "on the first of the Shabaths," - in the *count* to Shabuoth. There were many lamps in the upper room where they were listening to Paul speak. It was night, and Paul spoke until midnight. This is not teaching anyone to observe the rising Sun deity's steeple meetings, but clearly twisted by men inventing their own methods of worship.

www.fossilizedcustoms.com/syncretism.html

Do You Eat Pigs?

We may eat what is set-apart by the Word. If pigs are not set-apart by the Word as food, we don't eat their flesh, or touch their carcasses. YashaYahu 66:17 describes the catastrophic end for those whose works (behavior) involves eating unclean animals.

LET NO ONE INCRIMINATE YOU

"Therefore let no one **judge** (incriminate) you by what you eat or drink, or with regard to a feast, a new month, or a Shabath." These things are a shadow of things to come FOR the body of Mashiak. Although the translators and teachers of Kolossians 2:16-17 have made the impression that a shadow (an outline of a far more concrete objective) seems unimportant, the guarding of Yahuah's Word is what we Natsarim were commissioned to teach all the nations to guard, warning every man (Kolossians 1:28). Being disobedient is not the way to please Yahusha, we are to walk as He walked.
The one claiming to know Him must walk as He walked (1Yn. 2:6). Paul wrote about those who are deceptive workers:
"For such are malicious emissaries, deceptive workers, masquerading as emissaries of Mashiak. And no wonder! For shatan himself masquerades as a messenger of light! It is not surprising, then, if his servants also masquerade as servants of obedience, whose end shall be according to their works!"
2 Korinthians 11:13-15 **BYNV**

www.fossilizedcustoms.com/food.html

CHRISTOGRAMS
The Name of our Deliverer is feared by mankind's adversary. Satan knows, and shudders at Acts 4:12.
The one Name we are to call on is the real one, Yahusha. There is only one Name Satan fears: Yahusha. It turned the world upside down in the 1st century, and it is doing it all over the Earth again. Our fathers have inherited only lies and futility because our teachers have withheld the Truth from us.

Mystagogues devised ways of encrypting the names of their deities in the ancient world because they did not want outsiders to know them. This process elevated them in the eyes of the ignorant they wanted to control. The real Name was easy to hide as copies of Scripture were being made, and even easier when translated into foreign languages.
In the eastern Roman empire, **IC-XC** was used as a Christogram, and was representing the first and last letters in the Greek words *IESOUS* and *XRISTOS*, using the Latin **C** in place of the Greek letter sigma. In the western empire, **IESV** was used as a Christogram. **IHS** is another Christogram, using the uncial (capital) Greek letter **H** for epsilon, from the first 3 letters of iesous, itself another Christogram, or encryption.
Some have claimed an Egyptian trinity, Isis, Horus, and Seb were another influence for the **IHS** formulation, because Christianity's doctrinal *fathers* were headmasters at the Catechetical School of Alexandria, Egypt. A few pages ahead I will quote one of these headmasters, Epiphanius. The things he admits are stunning!
This school at Alexandria became known as the Didascalia (Greek for teaching authority), and the **Magisterium** (Latin for teaching authority). People are waking up to the fact that "JESUS" is not the real Name, but rather it is Yahusha. The NIV footnotes define it as "the lord is salvation." Those translators could have only looked to the Hebrew meaning (I am your Deliverer), because the Greek and Latin have no such meaning. **IESV** is a device, an invention used to to conceal, or stand-in as a replacement for the true Name, Yahusha. IESV is Pastors are admitting they have been deceived. A retired pastor in his 80's called me once, admitting he had been leading people astray for decades, and wanted to ask me what he should do now. I told him to find water, and go into it calling on the Name, Yahusha, for the forgiveness of his crimes, and teach that Name,

and teach others to obey everything He commanded. Yahusha is the Ruach ha Qodesh, Al Shaddai; anyone that has seen Yahusha has seen Yahuah. "I am He," these words caused them all to fall backward. Who do you say Yahusha is?
http://www.fossilizedcustoms.com/secretidentity.html

At Acts 15:21 it says gentiles can hear the Turah read in the synagogues in every city **every Shabath**. There's much more written about the weekly day we rest, as well as the festivals ignored by Christianity. Hebrews 4 mentions resting on the 7th, or we are being disobedient for a lack of belief. Shabath is the sign of the eternal Covenant of Love (favor). Let's just rest when Yahuah told us to, and call on His true Name, Yahusha. Why does this seem impossible? Natsarim are a threat to the dragon's authority, which is expressed in men's teachings which keep changing. Yahuah's Word is a solid foundation; traditions of men are sliding around. Rev. 12:17 describes the dragon's rage at those who obey the Commandments of Alahim, and hold to the testimony of Yahusha. The dragon and all who obey his lies are being warned over and over; the one you obey is the one you are the servant of (Romans 6:16). As for me and my house, we serve Yahuah. All who join to Yahuah, guarding His Shabath, are welcome to His Mishkan (YashaYahu / Isaiah 56). Those outside will gnash their teeth.
www.fossilizedcustoms.com/sabbath.html

This we know: Shabath will be the 4th Commandment forever. It was outlawed by Constantine, and at the Council of Laodicea (370 CE) those guarding the 4th Commandment were anathema, worthy of death.
And yet, in the last days, Yahusha told us to pray our flight not be on a Shabath (Mt. 24:20). YashaYahu / Isaiah 24 describes the reason Yahuah will burn the entire Earth: **the inhabitants transgressed the everlasting Covenant, and Shabath is the sign of that Covenant between Yahuah and His people forever.**

What Is A Worship Service?
"'And in vain do they worship Me, teaching as teachings the commands of men.' Forsaking the command of Alahim, you hold fast the tradition of men. And He said to them, 'Well do

you set aside the command of Alahim, in order to guard your tradition.'" - Mark 7:8-9 BYNV

True worship is **obedience**, but this understanding has been programmed-away, and thought of as **assembling for services.** The Shabath yom is primarily for us to rest in all our dwellings, staying in our place (Ex. 16:29-30). There is even a **"Shabath distance"** mentioned by Luke at Acts 1:12. As incredible as it may be, we are not *compelled* to assemble together but 3 times in a year, but *we are free to assemble every day* if we have the opportunity. Where ever 2 or 3 are gathered in Yahusha's Name, He is there (Mt. 18:20 eliminating the idea of a minyan of 10).

The assembly is where we hear the Word read, and each one may have a revelation, an interpretation, psalm, or teaching to share for the edification of all present. (1 Kor. 14:26)
http://www.fossilizedcustoms.com/Sabbath_Worship.html

Miqara means *to proclaim* (QARA), and the Turah was taught by reading it aloud. In the small villages all over the ancient world, this enabled the assemblies of converts to hear it read, but every person in town that had already had been raised in Turah was never the objective. The little rooms would not hold very many people. At Philippi, Paul attended a customary meeting-place on the Shabath with Lydia and other notable women by a river (Acts 16:13). When available to teach, elders would volunteer to read The Turah, Nabim, and Kathubah. At Exodus / Shemoth 16, in the training stages about the Shabath, everyone was to stay in their place. There's no mention of reading anything, only resting, and the priests were doing so many things there was no time or room to spare for them to be doing anything outside of their own duties in the center of the camp. Today we see bells, **steeples**, pews, pulpits and choirs everywhere in the world, because people have set aside the Commandments of Yahuah, and hold fast to their own traditions. (Click on the photo below to watch a youtube video)
Acts 15:21 tells us the guyim (gentiles) could progress further by hearing Mushah read in the assemblies **"every Shabath."** Those who attended these were mostly illiterate foreigners, and devout Yahudim seeking to help teach them.
No collections or basket-passing was going on.

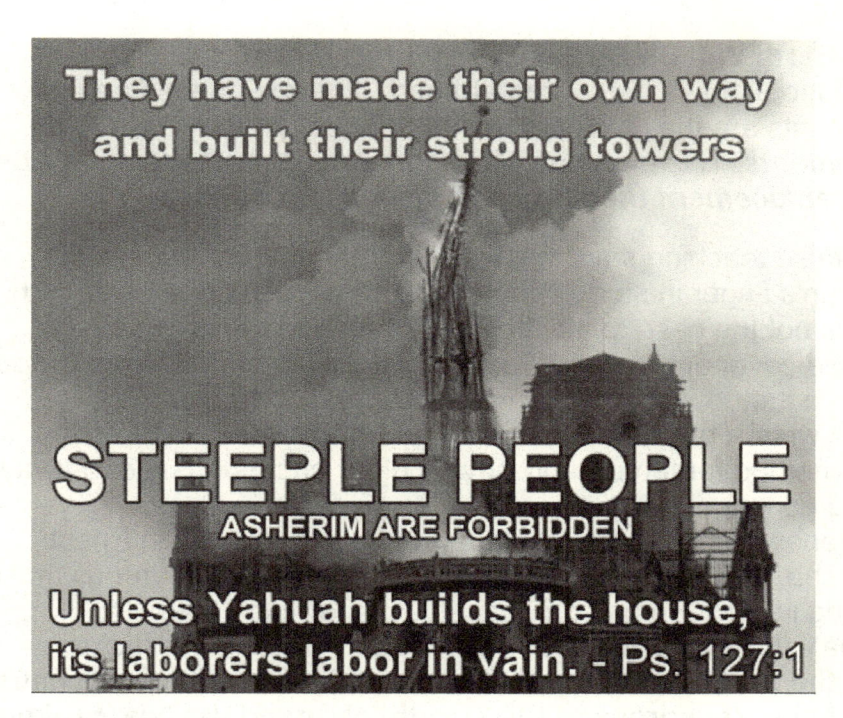

They have made their own way and built their strong towers

STEEPLE PEOPLE
ASHERIM ARE FORBIDDEN

Unless Yahuah builds the house, its laborers labor in vain. - Ps. 127:1

Shabath Misdirection-Trigger: Hebrews 4
"Everyday is a Sabbath" is heard over and over, all over the world. When we look for evidence proving *"everyday is a Sabbath"* in Scripture, it cannot be found. Instead, we find the specific day mentioned 9 times in the book of Acts, written by Luke about 22 years after Yahusha ascended. In His warnings about the signs of His return at Mt. 24:20, Yahusha told us through His first Natsarim to pray our flight would not be in winter, or on a Shabath yom. Obviously, He did not mean everyday, but the day we do not buy and sell, which is the sign of the eternal Covenant between Yahuah and His people. After Yahusha returns, prophecy tells us from *month to month, and Shabath to Shabath*, all flesh will obey Yahuah (see YashaYahu / Is. 66:23).

If *every day* is a Sabbath according to men's teachings, they are not the same as Yahuah's Shabaths, which He gave to us as a sign forever (see Ez. 20:12). We rest as Yahuah rested on the 7th day: Heb. 4:9: **"There remains, then, a Sabbath-rest for the people of Alahim; for anyone who enters Alahim's rest also rests from their works, just as Alahim did from His."**

www.fossilizedcustoms.com/sabbath.html

Why Earth Will Be Burned
Most people have been programmed to believe the old and new covenants are the divided portions of Scripture they refer to as *testaments*. This division is *Marcionism*, easily researched along with *replacement theology* and *dispensationalism*.

This false teaching says the Ten Commandments written with Yahuah's finger in stone tablets have now been done-away with. This is not the case at all, the Ten Commandments are eternal. The old covenant was the Turah (instruction) to offer **animal blood** through the now-obsolete priesthood (Hebrews 8:13).
It was written on a **scroll** and placed **beside** the ark (Dt. 31:26). That method for temporarily covering our crimes has faded away, and is no longer valid.
The renewed Covenant is through our permanent High Priest Yahusha, and the one-time offering of His own blood, for all those trusting in Him. He has purchased us; see Acts 20:28.
YashaYahu 24:5-6 tells us why the Earth will be devastated:
"For the arets has been defiled under its inhabitants, because they have transgressed the Turoth, changed the law, broken the everlasting covenant. Therefore a curse shall consume the arets, and those who dwell in it be punished."
Reapers are waiting to be released a day Yahuah has set.
www.fossilizedcustoms.com/reapers.html

When all Scripture is taken together as inspired by the same Being, everything is consistent with reality. All creation bears the evidence of creation's Designer, and many are called by Him to draw closer and learn His ways, and teach others. Men twist Scripture to fit their own ideas, and others pick up their teachings and spread the wormwood far and wide. Men's traditions grow like leaven, and are very religious as they seek to control beliefs. Yahusha comes into us to purge out that old leaven, and teach us the goal is love.
www.fossilizedcustoms.com/religion.html

Teachers are the primary source of confusion. They bring what they already believe to their study of Yahuah's Word, forcing it to mean things they want it to be saying. This is called *eisegesis*, reading things into the text that are not being taught, but hunting for proof of what is already believed. The opposite of this is to let the Word teach us, and taking in the surrounding context to determine what is being taught. This is called *exegesis*.

Hebrews 4 uses the word *rest* in association with the words "seventh" and "day" at 4:4, and resting from our own works just as Yahuah rested from His is what the text is teaching us. We show our belief or unbelief by our works, so others may see our good works and praise our Father. Resting cannot be work, but the opposite of work. Obedience to the Commandments of Alahim enrages the dragon (Rev. 12:17), not Yahusha. We are to walk as He walked, not be disobedient. We are the servant of the one we obey (Romans 6:16), and listen to my Shepherd, not Constantine.

The adoption of the day of the Sun as practiced from 321 CE onward (see Edict of Constantine) as a day to rest was originally established to honor Sol Invictus (Apollo), and later reinforced at the council of Laodicea. I love the Commandments, as they are written. Let's do the Word, not men's traditions. Why would Yahusha warn us about the last days, and to pray our flight not be on a Shabath at Mt. 24:20? If eisegesis is used to implant the idea that *Yahush is our rest,* then why do Christians *rest* on Sunday? It's about money!

The spelling JEHO seems preferred over **YAHU** because in the 8th century the Masoretes inserted phonemes (speech guides) to influence the way to pronounce words. They are called *niqqud marks*, yet no such marks are found on any of the Dead Sea Scrolls because all the vowels are written letters. The Name Yahuah is written with four Hebrew vowels, and as our Deliverer a suffix is used (shin-ayin) producing YAHU+SHA (yod-hay-uau + shin-ayin).
More evidence is here: **www.fossilizedcustoms.com/name.html**

FISCUS JUDAICUS

Few today have heard of the **Fiscus Judaicus**, a tax on those practicing Turah after the destruction of Yerushalayim that went on for centuries. The pressure to invent new practices and a different name for themselves was mostly based on avoiding this tax. They turned away from all practices that could be used as evidence they were serving Yahuah; the dragon left them alone.
A new teaching authority began at Alexandria, Egypt about 190 CE, known as the **Didascalia** (literally meaning *teaching authority*). This school (ecole) was also known as the **Catechetical School at Alexandria,** (C.S.A.).

Seminaries teach the writing of these fathers of the circus (kirke). The church (circus) fathers regarded the Natsarim as heretics mainly for rejecting the ecclesiastical power of their teaching authority, and holding instead to the Commandments of Yahuah as the final authority.
We recall that Yahusha was asked by what authority He was teaching and doing the things He did (Mt. 21:23).
Teaching authorities tend to only recognize **teachers** and **teachings** they endorse, and dismiss all others as false, often persecuting others to death.
This was the outcome for their hatred of Yahusha, and their primary motivation.
"They shall put you out of the congregations, but an hour is coming when everyone who kills you shall think he is rendering service to Alahim.
And this they shall do to you because they did not know the Father, nor Me. **-** Yahukanon / John 16:2-3
Natsarim do not kill people, but they are spoken against everywhere:
Acts 28:22: **"And we think it right to hear from you what you think, for indeed, concerning this sect, we know that it is spoken against everywhere."**

The 4th-century circus father Epiphanius **saw** the Hebrew text of MatithYahu used by one of the Natsarim he had encountered. Also, a Hebrew copy of MatithYahu (Matthew) was discovered in the DSS, which was preserved in cave 1 because it had the Name written on the parchment. Yahuah is our Deliverer, which is what YAHUSHA means. Epiphanius wrote this about an encounter with one of the Natsarim, a sect he considered to be heretics:
"We shall now especially consider heretics who call themselves Natsarim; they are mainly Yahudim and nothing else. They make use not only of the New Testament, but they also use in a way the Old Testament of the Yahudim; for they do not forbid the books of the Law, the Prophets, and the Writings... so that they are approved of by the Yahudim, from whom the Natsarim do not differ in anything, and they profess all the dogmas pertaining to the prescriptions of the Law and to the customs of the Yahudim, except they believe in Messiah. They preach that there is but one God, and His Son Yahusha the Messiah. But they are very learned in the Hebrew

language; for they, like the Yahudim, read the whole Law, then the Prophets...They differ from the Yahudim because they believe in Messiah, and from the Christians in that they are to this day bound to the Yahudim rites, such as circumcision, the Sabbath, and other ceremonies. They have the Good news according to Matthew in its entirety in Hebrew. For it is clear that they still preserve this, in the Hebrew alphabet, as it was originally written."

Obviously, Epiphanius **would** forbid the Law, Prophets, and Writings (TaNaK), often referred to by Yahusha. The Shabath observance (a day blessed at Creation) was observed by Yahusha, yet those who walk as He walked are heretics. This record hits on how doctrinally arrogant things had become very early, and why Christian doctrines are so different from the first followers of Yahusha. After Irenaeus, a new heretical error crept-in called **Apostolic Succession** along with the idea that the church hierarchy could supersede any Commandment, and usurp the name Israel (**Yisharal**) for itself. There is evidence that the Natsarim Sect continued to exist until at least the 13th century.

The Catholic writings of **Bonacursus** entitled **Against the Heretics** refers to **Nazarenes,** who were also called Pasagini. Bonacursus says,

"Let those who are not yet acquainted with them, please note how perverse their belief and doctrine are. First, they teach that we should obey the Law of Moses according to the letter - the Sabbath, and circumcision, and the legal precepts still being in force. Furthermore, to increase their error, they condemn and reject all the Church Fathers, and the whole Roman Church."

We were still around in the 13th century. Indeed, we Natsarim still obey that Old Law (the Ten Commandments, as written), and we still *"reject all the church fathers, and the whole Roman church."* We are accused of being *Jewish*, but we are really made up of **all** the lost tribes in captivity among the nations, as the Prodigal Son found himself and returned to the Covenant, the Father's household (Turah). We love all the household of belief. In fact, we are those described at Rev 12 & 14;

1. We **hold to the testimony of Yahusha** (we confess Yahusha and live according to what He taught), and
2. We **obey the Commandments of Yahuah**.
For this behavior we are branded as perverse heretics.
Much more research is available here:
www.fossilizedcustoms.com/natsarim.html

OTHER NAMES FOR NATSARIM OVER THE AGES
Several of the "fathers" of the Catechetical school at Alexandria mentioned the Natsarim, calling them heretics. They referred to the Natsarim as: Nazaraioi (men of Nazareth), Ebionites (poor ones), Waldenses/Waldensians (valley-dwellers), Valdus, Waldo, Albigenses (exterminated by the Inquisition in the town of Albi, France, were called **Cathars** – or *pure or clean ones*), Toulousians, and Pasagians (who believed in obedience to the "old law," their name meaning *passage*).
They wrote of their behavior of reading the Turah and prophets, circumcising their male children, keeping the appointed times, and being of no difference from the Yahudim, except that they believed in the Mashiak. While holding **obedience** against the Natsarim (called legalism in modern times), the circus fathers would self-castrate themselves! They were over-hauling things out of their own pagan imaginations. Recall that Danial asked the chief of the eunuchs if the young men with him could eat only vegetables. The young men from Yerushalom were castrated, and placed with the head of the eunuchs and educated in the ways of Babel, and this included Danial himself.

Yahuah gave this as His first order to the man & woman:
"Be fruitful and multiply."

Pagans have been focusing on castrating people
And aborting children.
One would wonder who they are obeying.

ORIGEN: SELF-CASTRATED HEADMASTER
The young men on the right of this picture are not sun-bathing. Self-castration was a common practice at the **Didascalia** a Greek word meaning teaching authority.
Magisterium is the Latin word for teaching authority.
Natsarim is the Hebrew term for branches, and depending on the context can also mean guardians or watchmen. The word also means branches, as descendants of the *teachings* of Yahusha ha Mashiak. Natsarim are prophesied at YirmeYahu 31:6 to rise on the hills of Afraim. We are mentioned at Acts 24:5 as Paul was called a **"ringleader of the sect of the Natsarim."** The word Nazarene is a misspelled word, there's no letter Z, it's TS, the Hebrew letter known as TZADEE. ZAYIN is not in the word.

CHRISTIANOS: CALLED AN IDIOT AT ANTIOCH
Yahusha's first followers were referred to by outsiders as *christianos*, a *term of scorn* meaning *idiots* at first in Antioch. Google the etymological source of the word cretin, and you will see it stems from *christianos.* Notice this label in context with *suffering* from the accusation of being called by this term:
"For do not let any of you suffer as a murderer, or thief, or doer of evil, or as a meddler. But if one suffers being a christianos,

let him not be ashamed, but let him esteem Alahim in this matter." 1Peter 4:15-16

Natsarim are indwelled by the Spirit of Yahusha. They are referred to as the bride, first-fruits, chosen ones, the higher-calling, and they guard the Commandments of Alahim and hold to the testimony of Yahusha (Rev. 12, Rev. 14).

Natsarim are all priests (kohenim), our Head is Yahusha, not a man. We don't practice infant immersions. We circumcise our male infants on the 8th day, just as Yahusha was. We walk as Yahusha walked, and don't use bones (relics), indoor altars or even buildings to worship Yahuah. We are His Mishkan (Temple).

EARLY COUNCILS OF DOOM
INHERITING FALSEHOOD FROM OUR FATHERS
TORAH INSTITUTE

NATSARIM - NO WITCHCRAFT

Natsarim don't **bow** to images or matsah displayed in a monstrance, nor do we **pray to the dead** (even Yahusha's mother, Miryam) - that's *idolatry, necromancy, and divination*. Natsarim don't use rosaries, that would be **divining** through necromancy. Some kneel to bread over which a fellow uttered the Latin words, *"hoc est corpus meum,"* violating the first and second Commandments. Some trust in **holy water**, and are practicing witchcraft. Holy water is not real, it's imaginary nonsense. Catholicism adopted it from the Hindu belief in sacred water from the Ganges River. These things are sobering and perhaps horrifying to hear, but there is much, much more: scapulars, statues, indulgences from suffering in an imaginary place called Purgatory, - none of these things are of the Truth. They are **witchcraft**. Yahusha calls-forth a bride at His coming that has not been kissing the toes of statues, nor is she drunken on any schemes of the devil. Her behavior (garments) are not wrinkled for having rolled around on the ground with pagan behavior. We guard and teach His Commandments. You may investigate who the Natsarim are and see vile things being said about us. We expose lies, and have the highest of hopes for everyone. We do not shame them into the proper path, we simply plant the seeds of love into every kind of soil we pass by. Yahusha changes the hearts that receive His Word (seed), we only plant and water that seed. The Turah of kindness teaches us how to **love Yahuah**, and **love our neighbor**.

Praying to saints that have died is much less productive than speaking to saints that are **still alive**. There are saints (qodeshim, set-apart ones) living on the Earth *right now*, and we are ambassadors through whom Yahuah pleads for everyone to be restored to favor to Himself:

"And all matters are from Alahim, who has restored us to favor with Himself through Yahusha Mashiak, and has given us the service of restoration to favor, that is, that Alahim was in Mashiak restoring the world to favor unto Himself, not reckoning their trespasses to them, and has committed to us the word of restoration to favor. Therefore we are envoys on behalf of Mashiak, as though Alahim were pleading through us. We beg, on behalf of Mashiak: Be restored to favor with Alahim. For He made Him who knew no sin to be sin for us, so that in Him we might become the righteousness of Alahim." 2Kor 5:18-21

OUR COMMISSION IS TO TEACH OTHERS TO OBEY
The Covenant, the Ten Commandments of kindness, teaches us how to love. We are not taught, nor do we act in any way that is intended to persecute, slander, intimidate, or harm anyone.

Our sword is the Word of Yahuah, always wielded with the goal of love. The fruits of Yahusha's Spirit are seen in our behavior:
Love, joy, peace, patience, kindness, goodness, gentleness, faithfulness, and self-control (Galatians 5:22-23 & 1 Korinthians 13).
Love [AHABAH] is a verb, not a feeling. It means *actively helping others*.
When Yahusha said we are to love our neighbor as ourselves, and do to them as we would have them do to us, He was retraining our broken, self-centered hearts to think of others more highly than ourselves. His Spirit is given to those who obey, and if everyone saw the purpose of the Covenant, it would rise to the level of nation-states that would treat one another just as Yahuah intended.
To pray for world peace is to pray for the Covenant of Kindness to be accepted, and allowing Yahusha's Spirit to circumcise a love for them on every heart.
The power is not in the rules themselves, but in Yahusha who indwells hearts.
Our heart refers to our inner self; the vessel, lamp, or wineskin that submits itself to obey "from the heart."
"Not by might, nor by power, but by My Spirit" (Zek 4:6) teaches us to rely on Yahusha to supply the needs of His servants who wait for His appearing. His Word changes hearts.
Romans 12 describes Natsarim behavior.

We Have Inherited Hindu Behavior
Domes, prayer beads, holy water (Ganges River), crescents, mats (sacred spaces), yoga (yoking with demonic entities), necromancy (praying to the dead), and divination (like Tarot cards), halos, tea leaves, ancestor relics, ashes on foreheads, scrying, palm readings, images, bowing / namaste, candle-lighting, indoor altars, etc., are just a few of the Nimrod behavior we've inherited. *Arrogant nonsense* is how Peter describes the defilements of the world system:
"For speaking arrogant nonsense, they entice – through the lusts of the flesh, through indecencies – the ones who have indeed escaped from those living in delusion, promising them freedom, though themselves being slaves of corruption – for one is a slave to whatever overcomes him. For if after they have escaped the defilements of the world through the knowledge of the Master and Deliverer Yahusha Mashiak, they are again

entangled in them and overcome, the latter end is worse for them than the first. For it would have been better for them not to have known the way of righteousness, than having known it, to turn from the set-apart command delivered to them. For them the proverb has proved true, 'A dog returns to his own vomit,' and, 'A washed sow *returns* to her rolling in the mud.'"
- 2Pet. / Kefa 2:18-22

Another interesting item that shows **syncretism** has occurred: Catholics adopted *prayer beads* from the far east, or Buddhist traditions, and in turn passed these on the the Arabs via Islam.

The origin of these **repetitive prayer beads** is Shiva worship from Hinduism. India's realm reached the Middle East around 200 BCE, and it had established a trade route called the Silk Road. Caravans brought silk, incense, and many other wares out of India, along with their form of worshipping the host of heaven.

Domes, circumambulation, and shivaling inside shrines led by gurus, prayer mats, a *sacred space* for performing **yoga**, the *yoking* exercises which are performed by taking the shape of a crescent moon, and the bead-praying which were the **tears of Shiva**.

You may not like this information, but it's all Truth. You will see the images of Shiva depict the crescent, the beads, the serpent, and the Shivaling. More details on these is found in the book ***Who Is Allah?*** Masons worship Nimrod in shrines, and are the great builders of the domes in the western cultures. Shrine prostitutes *serviced* their patrons using full-body coverings to conceal their identity. See 1 Kings 14, and Gen. 38; this was the way Tamar concealed her identity from Yahudah, producing Perets and Zerah.

REFORMATION OR RESTORATION?

The dragon has divided the whole world against itself, and caused everyone to disobey Yahuah. Without Turah, the world is filled with a lack of love.

The Natsarim are a restoration. We are repairers of the breach, and work to restore the Covenant by sharing it with all people.

It's about love, not condemnation.

"And those from among you shall build the old waste places. You shall raise up the foundations of many generations. And you would be called the repairer of the breach, the restorer of streets to dwell In. If you do turn back your foot from the

Shabath, from doing your pleasure on My set-apart *day*, and shall call the Shabath 'a delight,' the set-apart day of Yahuah 'esteemed,' and shall esteem it, not doing your own ways, nor finding your own pleasure, nor speaking your own words, then you shall delight yourself in Yahuah. And I shall cause you to ride on the heights of the earth, and feed you with the inheritance of Yaqub your father. For the mouth of Yahuah has spoken!" YashaYahu / Is. 58:12-14

Yahusha has opened our hearts and minds to the Scriptures and the mission of love. www.fossilizedcustoms.com/tenvirgins.html

The word *didascalia* means *teaching authority*.
Natsarim do not recognize any **yoke** (teachings) but that of Yahusha.
We Natsarim love people, but share the Truth to tear down strongholds they may have (false reasoning). The Catechetical School at Alexandria is also called the Didascalia, and from there all Catholics and Protestants inherit their doctrinal errors from the kirke [church] fathers. The Natsarim teaching Authority is the living Spirit of Yahusha Who indwells us, and we don't have sacraments, ring-kissing, stoles, or a liturgy.

We don't have many things, but we guard and teach the Ten Commandments to all mankind. Just for fun, here's one thing we don't teach: It's a little dogma about a *stuffed donkey*:
   http://www.fossilizedcustoms.com/stuffeddonkey.html

Paul spoke about his former way of life in Yahudaism, the traditions of men, at Galatians 1:13-14. Those traditions were the yoke our fathers could not bear (Acts 15:10). He rejected all that, but never taught against obeying Yahuah's instructions for living. Paul warned us at 1Timothy 1:7 about teachers who have no idea what they are talking about. At Romans 3:31 Paul says we establish the Turah. The source of the 613 laws people talk about is the Talmud, an uninspired 1200+ year written record. The 613 represent the yoke of Rabbinic Yahudaism, most of which pertained to the old priesthood's animal blood work, added due to transgressions. Within those 613 instructions is the everlasting Covenant, which Yahuah inscribed with His finger in stone tablets. Aside from all the measured offerings of the priesthood, some were only for men, others for women, some about Nazir oaths. Yahusha could not obey an instruction only for women to obey, so by the time those 613 laws are whittled away to the bare essentials, what is left is a light yoke. If we turn our ear away from hearing His Turah, our prayers to Yahuah are an abomination to Him. (Proverbs 28:9; see also "the end of the matter," Eccl. 12:13-14)

ORIGINAL NATSARIM - Greek or Hebrew?

It is overwhelmingly evident the first followers of Yahusha wrote in Hebrew. An important bit of evidence is the Dead Sea Scrolls which contained a copy of the memior/gospel of MatithYahu written in Hebrew (Cave 1). There is evidence in the Natsarim text the language and alphabet of the writers was Hebrew.

The Hebrew tongue (language) is mentioned 3 times in the book of Acts: 21:40, 22:2, and 26:14.

Idioms (often called Hebraisms) are richly sprinkled throughout the Greek Received Text (Textus Receptus).

We also have the outside evidence from the circus fathers' writings.

HEBREW LANGUAGE – PROOF

Did Yahusha speak Hebrew, or Aramaic?

Act 26:14: **"And when we had all fallen to the ground, I heard a voice speaking to me, and saying in the Hebrew language, 'Shaul, Shaul, why do you persecute Me? It is hard for you to kick against the prods.'"**

This is one of 3 places we know He spoke **Hebrew.**

(See also Acts 21:40 & 22:2)

The word *Hebrew* is found 11 times in the First Natsarim Writings.

The 4th century circus father Epiphanius wrote about the Natsarim, and the **Hebrew language** they were fluent in speaking and writing.

In his doctrinal book, **_Against Heresies_**, Epiphanius wrote:

"The Natsarim do not differ in any essential thing from them [the Yahudim]**, since they practice the customs and doctrines prescribed by loudismos law; except that they believe in Christ. They believe in the resurrection of the dead, and that the universe was created by Theos. They preach that Theos is One, and that IESV Christos is his Son. They are very learned in the**

Hebrew language. They read the Turah. Therefore they differ from the TRUE Christians because they fulfill until now Ioudismos rites as the circumcision, Sabbath, and others."

[End quote from the Church Father Epiphanius in his doctrinal book, *Against Heresies*, Page 41, 402]

The circus father **Jerome** also encountered a Natsari, relating similar behavior in him. Obeying the popes, Catholic armies of Germany, France, and Bohemia brutally massacred their own population for centuries.

PERSECUTION / MASSACRE - 12TH CENTURY:

WALDENSIANS NAMED HERETICS BY POPE INNOCENT III

THE WIKIPEDIA ENCYCLOPEDIA STATES:

The Roman Catholic Church declared them heretics — stating the group's principal error was **"contempt for ecclesiastical power".**

The Waldensians were also accused by the Catholic Church of teaching ***innumerable errors.***

On the 24TH of the (4TH Roman month) 1655, at 4 am, the signal was given for a general massacre, the horrors of which can be detailed only in small part.

This massacre was so brutal, it aroused indignation throughout Europe. This brutality was ordered by the papacy againstHuguenots, the term used for the Natsarim, Yahusha's people. May Yahusha forgive them, they did not know what they were doing.

THE CATECHETICAL SCHOOL AT ALEXANDRIA
DISTINGUISHES NATSARIM AS DIFFERENT FROM THEMSELVES

Epiphanius – Headmaster at the CSA / Didascalia:

A 4th-century church father, gave a detailed description of the Natsarim:

"We shall now especially consider heretics who ... call themselves Natsarim; they are mainly Yahudim and nothing else. They make use not only of the New Testament, but they also use in a way the Old Testament of the Yahudim; for they do not forbid the books of the Turah, the Prophets, and the Writings... so that they are approved of by the Yahudim, from whom the Natsarim do not differ in anything, and they profess all the dogmas pertaining to the prescriptions of the Turah and to the customs of the Yahudim, except they believe in Mashiak.

They preach that there is but one Alahim, and His Son Yahusha the Mashiak.

But they are very learned in the Hebrew language; for they, like the Yahudim, read the whole Turah, then the Prophets ...

They differ from the Yahudim because they believe in Mashiak, and from the Christians in that they are to this day bound to the Yahudim rites, such as circumcision, the Sabbath, and other ceremonies. They have the Good news according to Matthew in its entirety in Hebrew. For it is clear that they still preserve this, in the Hebrew alphabet, as it was originally written."

[Origen, CSA / DIDASCALIA CIRCUS FATHER]

Try to imagine Yahusha being disgusted over anyone who obeys the Ten Commandments as written, and teaching them to others. He is the One that circumcises hearts with them, and could not possibly ever say, *"You're a legalist, and you're trying too hard to obey the Ten Commandments!"*

Natsarim are **fanatical** about their love for Yahusha, and are not lukewarm.

Yahusha is the Spirit Indwelling us, and He is our Armor. In the power of His Love we are enabled to overcome the world.

(beast organism's world order)

Practically everything we see and hear from teachers on any subject is a different spin on how to interpret Yahusha's will. Are we hearing His point of view, or that of the flesh? We must listen for His Voice in those who teach, and discern if we are hearing Him, or another shepherd (like the enemy's ministers of disobedience).

We are vessels of Yahusha, restoring lost sheep to His **eternal Covenant**.

Yahusha doesn't have *dispensations* of any kind. **He is the same yesterday, today, and forever.** His Word (Turah) will never pass away. The discussions we hear about *Dispensationalism* or *Replacement Theology* are not His Voice, but another's voice trying to provide excuses for not obeying.

Yahusha's point of view is all we need to hear from any teacher because His Word is not to be privately interpreted.

Whenever He sees a life, He sees love. We should view one another as He does, and our behavior between one another will reflect what we are **capable of becoming**, not what we may be in the moment. We are on the narrow path being guided by Yahusha, and are all under His blood, forgiven a great debt we could never repay. Let's not judge one another, and be tender-hearted toward all.

Love one another as He loves us, <u>always</u>.

He loved and died for us while we were yet criminals - we should commit our lives to rescue those around us even if it is without words.

Our behavior toward one another is the most powerful message of all - love. We are branches (Natsarim) of Yahusha Himself, His body, and He's looking for fruits to appear on us. We are Yahusha walking in this dark world.

The MEDIA is sometimes referred to as the *fourth estate.*
What are the first three?
The New World (Americas) has become an extension of the Old World Authority (Order), which is controlled as the Medieval Age was:
Clergy (now the Societas Iesu),
Nobility (governing authorities, and
Laity (commoners, the people).
The media is now a fourth estate, steered by the dragon.

Can Sacraments Help Save You?
Sacraments are the beast's primary means of control, wielded by the great harlot, and are nothing more than the imaginary incantations of a sorceress.
To keep the Nobility (2nd estate) in-line, the Clergy (1st estate) withholds the imaginary sacraments until they follow orders. The control is paper-thin, and the world economy is resting on all the fertility festivals everyone pretends are real. Babel (World Order) cannot be fixed or reformed, all one can do is come out of it by ignoring it. Those obedient to Yahusha hear Him saying, **"Come out of her, My people"** and this will cause all the merchants to wail, because no one will buy their merchandise anymore, just as we see written at Revelation 18.

The New World Order is the BEAST organism fully developed, which is the reign of Babel, the head of the statue revealed to Danial. Another reign, that of the Creator, exists like wheat struggling to survive among weeds, and these two crops compete for sunlight.
At the harvest, one of these authorities is removed forever, and the other is given the reign.
The fifth estate is now here, and we bypass the control of the clergy over the world. Social media has enabled us free access to one another.

WHO ARE THE NATSARIM allows you to distinguish the original followers of Yahusha (who first settled at Antioch), with the Didascalia, or Catechetical School at Alexandria - which was funded by Rome's Fiscus Judaicus, a tax on any who observed Turah.
This state-supported **Didascalia** (literally teaching authority) grew into the dominant forms of Christianity seen today.
After the destruction of Yerushalayim in 70 CE, two teaching authorities emerged: The Pharisees and the Natsarim.
The dragon (controlling the **beast**, the **reign of Babel**) demands complete submission to its authority, so persecution of the Natsarim was severe. That controller is now being revealed, which will be destroyed at the coming of Yahusha.
The way to recognize the Natsarim is by what they teach and their behavior, by the living Spirit of Yahusha in them producing the fruits of His Spirit: love, joy, peace, patience, kindness, goodness,

gentleness, faithfulness, and self-control - against which there is no law (Galatians 5). In the end, there are two plants growing in the world: wheat and tares. Discover which teaching authority you've been listening to.

The 1st Commandment is:
"I am Yahuah your Alahim; have no other before My Face."

Is The KJV Without Errors?

The KJV is an Anglican Catholic translation of the Latin Vulgate into old English, and is riddled with misinterpreted Hebrew words and misunderstood idioms taken out of context. The context at Mal. 4:2 concerns those who "revere My Name," yet the Name of the Creator is not found in the KJV. "Shammash" can mean "Sun," but in the context at Malaki 4:2 the word should be translated "Servant." At Mt. 26:17, one cannot prepare for the Passover on the 15th day of the first month (which is the first day of Unleavened Bread). The Passover was slain on the 14th. The greatest mistake is the removal of the Name (Yod-Hay-Uau-Hay: YAHUAH) about 6,823 times, and following the traditions of men. The Hebrew tradition of avoiding the utterance of the Name and substituting "Adonai" (meaning LORD) was later followed by the Greek Kurios (LORD), and then the Latin Dominus (LORD), was propagated into the Anglican Catholic KJV as "LORD." The Hebrew word BAAL is LORD. Yahuah is my Shepherd, not Baal. There's much more, but research the translations before recommending them. Most English versions follow the KJV. It's first edition used a christogram in place of the Name Yahusha; it appears as IESV. This is not a name at all, it's not even related to any Hebrew word. Google these terms: fossilized customs kjv, or simply visit **www.fossilizedcustoms.com/kjv.html**

Psa 138:2: *"I bow myself toward Your set-apart Hekal, And give thanks to Your Name For Your kindness and for Your Truth; For You have made great Your Word, Your Name, above all."*
An important part of our **restoration** involves *calling* upon the Name of our Creator. His Name as written in ancient Hebrew letters is shown in following illustration, and how many times it's found:

TRANSLITERATIONS

	6,823	216	2	1
	YAHUAH	**YAHUSHA**	**YAHUSHUA**	**Y'SHUA**
HEBREW	ᴎY˰Z	OWY˰Z	OYWY˰Z	OYWZ
ARAMAIC	יהוה	יהושׁע	יהושׁוע	ישׁוע
GREEK	IAOUE	IHSOUS		
LATIN	IEHOUAH	IESU		

AT HEBREWS 4 AND ACTS 7 THE SAME GREEK LETTERING IS USED FOR "JOSHUA" AND "JESUS" - IHSOUS
THIS IS CONFIRMATION BOTH WERE CALLED YAHUSHA IN HEBREW
TORAH INSTITUTE

Our letters **U**, **V**, and **W** came from the sixth letter of the ancient Hebrew alef-beth, a letter shaped: **Y** (yet it is not our modern letter that looks like this).

This Hebrew letter became the Greek letter UPSILON, also shaped Y. The Latin form of this letter dropped the stem, changing the shape to V, but keeping the sound "OO" as in our modern "U". The word for "sword" in Latin letters is GLADI<u>V</u>S (NOTE THE U IS SHAPED AS A V).

Within the last 700 years, this letter shaped "V" with the sound of the double-O, "OO" (as in "school") developed into our modern letters U and later the double-U, written as W. The "double-U" is a new letter, and not a letter known to the Hebrew language. Note that in the words YAH<u>U</u>DAH and HALLEL<u>U</u>-YAH we find the letter UAU also. Please verify this using online encyclopedias and other sources.

The Tetragrammaton is therefore more accurately rendered as YHUH, standing for the 4 letters YOD-HAY-UAU-HAY.

If preferred, it can be expressed YHVH, as long as it is understood that the Latin V-shape is sounded as our modern U.

In the first edition of the KJV, they used the Latin Vulgate's **IESV** Ii the text in place of the real Name, Yahusha.
The picture shown below may be verified easily.

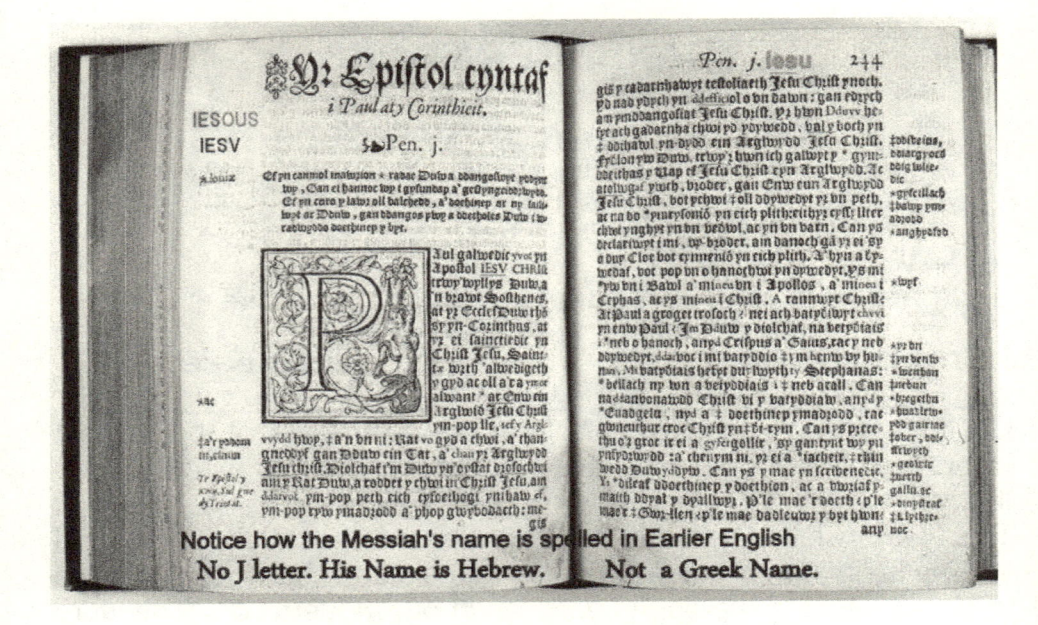

Notice how the Messiah's name is spelled in Earlier English
No J letter. His Name is Hebrew. Not a Greek Name.

BACK TO CONTENTS

Centuries Of Mistakes To Overcome
75 years after the printing of the Latin Vulgate by Gutenberg, William Tyndale published the Natsarim Writings from Greek into English (1526). In 1536, King Henry VIII arrested him and had him strangled and burned at the stake for his English publication which he smuggled into England from Germany. This was the first major effort to mass-produce the Scriptures in English.

The Adulterous Bible of 1631 seems to be telling us to adulterate:

> **ALTERING THE COMMANDS BY MISTAKE CAN HAPPEN**
>
> **The ADULTEROUS BIBLE**
> 1631 King James (Authorized Version)
>
> 12 ¶ * Honour thy father and thy mot
> thy dayes may bee long vpon the land
> LORD thy God giueth thee.
> 13 * Thou fhalt not kill.
> 14 Thou fhalt commit adultery.
> 15 Thou fhalt not fteale.
> 16 Thou fhalt not beare falfe witne
> thy neighbour
> 17 * Thou fhalt not couet thy nighbo
> thou fhalt not couet thy neighbours wif
>
> **BUT SHOULD NEVER BE DONE ON PURPOSE**
> **TORAH INSTITUTE**

A type-setter must have been very tired the day he was setting the type for Exodus 20:14 for a revised printing of the KJV. He made collectors extremely happy by leaving out the word "**not**."

The London printing firm was in big trouble over it. Another error is in this same printing; at Dt. 5:24, instead of referring to the "greatness" of (G-D), the typesetter inserted *"great-asse."* These incredible bloopers have caused a great uproar over the centuries.

www.fossilizedcustoms.com/bynv.html

Syncretism Explosion

Historically there have been many examples of blending together the Truth with false worship, and some Eberith cultures **called** on Yahuah and a consort / wife called **Asherah** even while they lived in the land given to them, according to the interpretations of archaeologists. During the period of the Shofetim (Judges) like Athnial, Shimshon, Deborah, and Gideon, Ali, Yefthah, Shemual, and others, the common people were easily tainted by the surrounding worshipers of the host of heaven. Worship of the creation rather than the Creator is still overwhelming the Guyim (nations). The main reason people are led astray is their teachers (YashaYahu / Isaiah 9:16), and their failure to check everything they are taught (2 Timothy 2:15). Today on the Internet, even a blending of scripts is being promoted everywhere. People tend to believe everything they hear, and fail to check to see if these things are so. **www.fossilizedcustoms.com/hyksoshoax.html**

The letters we see in Eberith or even Aramith contain the sounds of the four vowels, and Latin, Greek, and English fail us as we attempt any phonology. All we can do is write our understanding in phonetic form. In this and other videos, I attempt to show the original letters. The form **YEHOVAH** as we see often contains several new ideas, some from the added niqqud marks (767 CE and forward), and the shape of the Latin **V**, which was originally sounded as the Greek upsilon, and now our modern u. V in GLADI<u>V</u>S (GLADI<u>U</u>S) illustrates this. When we add the sound of the <u>modern</u> V to the Name, we involve the <u>upper teeth</u> and <u>lower lip</u>, disqualifying the letter as a <u>vowel</u>. If I am mistaken, please correct me on this: Yusef Ben MatithYahu (Flavius Josephus) said they were 4 <u>vowels</u>.

VOWEL: A vowel is a letter sounded <u>without</u> using the lips, teeth, upper teeth on lower lip, or tongue on the roof of the mouth; only the breath and mouth cavity are used.

CONSONANT: A consonant is a letter making use of the lips, teeth, upper teeth on lower lip, or tongue on the roof of the mouth. Psalm <u>118:26</u> is quoted by Yahusha at Mt. <u>23:39</u> when He said, "You will not see Me again until you say:

BARUK HABA BASHEM YAHUAH

Does Yahuah really not want anyone to call on His Name? This is not a hard answer to find. For example, this text is very clear: *"Pour out Your wrath on the guyim Who have not known You, And on reigns that have not called on Your Name."* (Psalm 79:6) Transliteration convey the **sound**, or phonology of letters and words. Translations convey the **meanings** of words, in their context. Be careful how you hear, and what you treasure in your heart. **"May the words of my lips and meditation in my heart be pleasing in Your sight Yahuah, my Rock and my Redeemer."** Ps. 19:14

The four letters of the Name are written **vowels**. To say **_YEHO_** expresses the influences of niqqud marks **_invented_** by the Masoretes, a sect of Karaites (E, O instead of A,U, YAHU).
The third letter of the Name is the same letter we hear in hallel **U** Yah.

What is a vowel, and what is a consonant?
VOWEL: A vowel is a letter sounded without using the lips, teeth, upper teeth on lower lip, or tongue on the roof of the mouth; only the breath and mouth cavity are used.
CONSONANT: A consonant is a letter making use of the lips, teeth, upper teeth on lower lip, or tongue on the roof of the mouth.
YEHOVAH as spoken by many is therefore incorrect on the basis of several misunderstandings. The V is being sounded in the modern world's understanding, using the upper teeth and lower lip, making it a consonant. The niqqud marks added during the 8th century by the Karaites altered the phonology from YAHU to YEHO, adding vowels to cue a reader to say another word, ADUNI (my lord).
Fact: the Dead Sea Scrolls have no phonemes added (niqqud marks). Eberith already has written vowels, ALEF (**A**), AYIN (**A** or **E**), HAY (**H**), UAU (**U** – having same shape and sound as the Greek letter UPSILON), YOD (**Y**; matching the Greek IOTA).
Flavius Josephus (Yusef Ben MatithYahu) knew the four letters of the Name he saw on the headpiece of the kohen ha gadol were vowels, and said so. This is confirmed later by a circus father at Alexandria named Clement, who transliterated the Name in these Greek letters: **IAOUE**, producing the phonetic sound, **YAHUAH** in our modern understanding.

63

Phonology is the study of the sound of a language. Yahuah used the language of Eber to inspire His prophets (Eberith aka Hebrew).

Traditions of men controlled who could teach, and what. When reading Word of Yahuah aloud, there has been a long-standing resistance to uttering the Name.

In the 8th century, a sophisticated method using vowel-marks was developed, and it has been promoted successfully for many centuries and is the official delusion now. It has been the primary lock keeping everyone from calling on the Name.

We have the Key, and we're the guardians of the Name.

The First Will Be Last (Mt. 19:30)
We are the **last** Natsarim, the restoration ambassadors teaching the same message as the **first** followers of Yahusha. The World Order (Clergy-Nobility-Laity) is crumbling, and the real message of the reign of Yahusha is enlightening people everywhere. Here in the last days, Yahusha is awakening His bride, those having stored up the extra oil of His Name. The conspiracy to conceal His Name *is* being shouted from the rooftops. The apostasy (*falling-away*) came first. (2 Thess. 2:3) Are you feeling the urges from Yahusha to fall away from men's teachings and learn Truth? Men's teachings are called leaven. One of the problems of getting to the Truth has always been a teaching authority stepping in to make it seem a *lay person* (laity, common people) doesn't have the capacity, training, or *permission granted* to them to teach. This was how they treated Yahusha, because He released so much Truth He became a threat to the fragile egos of those controlling teachings. Yahusha is our Teacher, not traditions invented by men. The **Name** is the Key of knowledge, the Rock rejected by the builders. (Ps. 118:26)

TRANSLITERATIONS

	6,823	216	2	1
	YAHUAH	**YAHUSHA**	**YAHUSHUA**	**Y'SHUA**
HEBREW	ayzi	owyzi	oywyzi	oywzi
ARAMAIC	יהוה	יהושׁ	יהושׁו	ישׁו
GREEK	IAOUE	IHSOUS		
LATIN	IEHOUAH	IESU		

AT HEBREWS 4 AND ACTS 7 THE SAME GREEK LETTERING IS USED FOR "JOSHUA" AND "JESUS" - IHSOUS
THIS IS CONFIRMATION BOTH WERE CALLED YAHUSHA IN HEBREW
TORAH INSTITUTE

First-Use Of The Hebrew Name Yahusha

Mushah invented this spelling; it's important to explain the origin (first use) of the spelling **yod-hay-uau-shin-ayin** in Hebrew. Mushah called Husha the son of Nun, *Yahusha* (Numbers 13:16) by adding a the letter YOD to his name.

This will also explain how a *transliteration* is different from a *translation* (a word's meaning brought over to a new language in its proper context). Husha is a *transliteration* (or trans-lettering) of the four Hebrew letters **hay-uau-shin-ayin**. Hebrew is read from right-to-left, and the illustration above will help show you the different scripts and how to pair them with their counterpart sounds in various other scripts.

Husha means *deliverer*. Adding the letter **Y** to the name **Husha** transformed it to *Yahusha,* meaning *I am your deliverer*.

The original name of the man Husha was diminished to form the suffix *SHA*, and the letter hay was absorbed to form YAHU (yod-hay-uau).

When we explain the sound of the letters, and say them clearly, Yahusha comes out clearly. It's just like Romans 10 says,

They must call on the Name to be delivered, and someone must be sent to speak to them.

From time to time we see books with strange substitutions for Alahim, such as G-D, or L-rd, because they don't make the effort to explain the Eberith / Hebrew word.

Photos of the NIV and NASB prefaces admit they substituted the Name with a device, LORD:

> **NIV - PREFACE**
>
> In regard to the divine name *YHWH*, commonly referred to as the *Tetragrammaton*, the translators adopted the device used in most English versions of rendering that name as "LORD" in capital letters to distinguish it from *Adonai*, another Hebrew word rendered "Lord," for which small letters are used. Wherever the two names stand together in the Old Testament as a compound name of God, they are rendered "Sovereign LORD."
>
> Because for most readers today the phrases "the LORD of hosts" and "God of hosts" have little meaning, this version renders them "the LORD Almighty" and "God Almighty." These renderings convey the sense of the Hebrew, namely, "he who is sovereign over all the 'hosts' (powers) in heaven and on earth, especially over the 'hosts' (armies) of Israel." For readers unacquainted with Hebrew this does not make clear the distinction between *Sabaoth* ("hosts" or "Almighty") and *Shaddai* (which can also be translated "Almighty"), but the latter occurs infrequently and is always footnoted. When *Adonai* and *YHWH Sabaoth* occur together, they are rendered "the Lord, the LORD Almighty."
>
> As for other proper nouns, the familiar spellings of the King James Version are generally retained.

> **The Proper Name of God in the Old Testament:** In the Scriptures, the name of God is most significant and understandably so. It is inconceivable to think of spiritual matters without a proper designation for the Supreme Deity. Thus the most common name for deity is God, a translation of the Hebrew *Elohim*. The normal word for Master is Lord, a rendering of *Adonai*. There is yet another name which is particularly assigned to God as His special or proper name, that is, the four letters YHWH (Exodus 3:14 and Isaiah 42:8). This name has not been pronounced by the Jews because of reverence for the great sacredness of the divine name. Therefore, it was consistently pronounced and translated LORD. The only exception to this translation of YHWH is when it occurs in immediate proximity to the word Lord, that is, *Adonai*. In that case it is regularly translated GOD in order to avoid confusion.
> — NASB - PRINCIPLES OF TRANSLATION

The two texts shown above explore this confusion with eyes shut. This book addresses the letters of the inspired text, how they sound and look, and the first-use of the Name above all names, Yahusha. People are able to learn if they are provided all the information.
If someone is limited to only partial or erroneous information, they may attempt to "call" on "Y-Husha" for their deliverance, and then we would have a new wind of doctrine start up, and spread everywhere to divide the body.
Recently someone wrote to me saying His Name is Ya*hayah*sha. I've never seen anything in the Eberith text constructed to produce such an arrangement, so it is most likely a teaching based on some transliterations con-*fusing* ahayah, Yahuah, and Yahusha. The Hebrew word *ahayah* is a verb meaning *I will be*. There are at least 6823 uses of the Name **Yahuah** between **Barashith** (Genesis) and **Malaki** (Malachi). **AliYahu** (Elijah) did not say *ahayah* at Mt. Karmel.

Is Our Creator's Name Yahuah or Ahayah?
Yahuah says this about His **Name** (not *Names*):
"I am Yahuah, that is My Name, and My esteem I do not give to another, nor My praise to idols." YashaYahu / Isaiah 42:8 BYNV
There are reasons AHAYAH is not the Name, but there is a fundamental grammatical reason it can't be.
Our word *noun* literally means the *name* of something. A noun is a **thing**, and describes **what** something is, not **what** it is doing, **why** it is doing it, **where** it is doing it, **when** it is doing it, or **how** it is doing it. His Name is not modifying or describing another word in a sentence because His Name always functions as the subject or object in the sentence, phrase, or clause.
A personal name is a **pronoun**, not an action word. AHAYAH is used in Yahuah's statement as a **verb**, and means *I will be* (exist);

therefore on the basis of it being used as a verb, it cannot be taken to be a pronoun (name).
People that may have been drawn into the false idea that EHYEH or AHAYAH is the true Name of our Creator have been misled, just as Paul said they would be at Acts 20:29.

Shemoth / Exodus 3:14, 15 in the Hebrew tells us **YOD-HAY-UAU-HAY** is His Name forever throughout all generations, and is the Name found at least 6,823 times in the TaNaK. The phrase *AHAYAH ASHER AHAYAH* is understood to mean "I will be Who I will be."
AHAYAH is not used in the phrase as a noun or name, but as a **verb** meaning *to exist*. In the conversation with Mosheh, Yahuah is telling him He **will be** Who He **is**, and He **will remain** Who He **is**. He then reveals the Name by which He will be known forever throughout all generations: **Yahuah**. Yahuah became flesh, and dwelled among us in the form of a man, and given the Name Yahusha by inspiration. Yahusha's renown is expressed in the word **Emanual**, meaning *Alahim is with us.* Renown refers to what something is known for. Yahusha is known to be Emanual. Yahusha is His *Name*, and Emanual *identifies Him to be Alahim.* This is the same case we see at YashaYahu (Isaiah) 9:6:
"For a Child shall be born to us, a Son shall be given to us, and the rule is on His shoulder. And His Name is called Wonder, Counsellor, Strong Al, Father of Continuity, Prince of Peace."

To think this is telling us His Name is Wonder, Ahayah, or Emanual is to miss the point. Yahuah tells us what His memorial Name is:
"And Alahim said further to Mushah, 'Thus you are to say to the children of Yisharal, "Yahuah Alahim of your fathers, the Alahim of Abraham, the Alahim of Yitshaq, and the Alahim of Yaqub, has sent me to you. This is My Name forever, and this is My remembrance to all generations." Shemoth / Exodus 3:15

Also, among 6,823 other places using the Name, we find:
"I am Yahuah, that is My Name, and My esteem I do not give to another, nor My praise to idols." YashaYahu (Isaiah) 42:8

NIMROD'S SECRET IDENTITY

SEE SERPENTS?

AUTHORITY OVER MEN TO RULE GIVEN BY THE DRAGON TO HIS SERPENT KINGS

FIRST DEIFIED SUPERMAN: **NIMROD**

TORAH INSTITUTE

ORIGIN OF WORD GOD *Super-human Nimrod, Superman*
The 1945 Encyclopedia Americana has this to say under to topic **GOD**:

"GOD (god); Common Teutonic word for personal object of religious worship, formerly applicable to super-human beings of heathen myth; on conversion of Teutonic races to Christianity, term was applied to Supreme Being."

This source refers directly to the characteristics of Nimrod, the first to become worshipped as a Sun deity, and all *Serpent Kings*. The fictional Superman is Nimrod, look closely at the logo, and the serpent is easily perceived. The eye is shown in all the logos.

SERPENT GOD   NIMROD

Astrology sprang from the Babel Roots, not the Hebrew Roots. Nimrod built Babel, and mankind has been drinking from the cup of Babel, and gone mad.
The English word GOTT was the Norse word for the Sun, and was their proper noun (personal name) for the object they worshipped. Woden's Daeg (Wednesday) is hiding Nimrod's name, babbled as Odin / Woden. Woden's symbol is the celtic crux. Natsarim do not refer to Yahuah by any pagan titles or names, they use His true Name, being careful to guard it and not allow it to be destroyed.
We have inherited nothing but lies and futility.
Try your best to get this book, it will show you the real secrets that have been kept from you by the dragon's teaching authorities:

FOSSILIZED CUSTOMS
THE BEAST IS UNVEILED
THE PAGAN ORIGINS OF POPULAR CUSTOMS
12th Edition
THE MOST COMPLETE BOOK OF SECRETS

To draw pupils away to follow them, teachers are using their *misunderstandings* of Scripture to divide and confuse, and they are identified by their false teachings. The less people study on their own, the easier it is for them to be led astray by every new idea that comes along. Idioms, metaphors, maxims, and parables can knock people *"for-a-loop."*

The fake name JESUS (or the other replacement names like ISA, IESV, IHS, IC-XC) follows the policy of pagan **mystagogues**. Mystagogues are real too, but few know about them. They conceal the true name of their deities, and their initiates (pupils) hold them in high esteem, not unlike a guru, rabbi, or master. They are still around. They have control over far more than people realize. The grading system of all teaching authorities on Earth practice their methodology. Masons could not function without keeping many secrets from the lower grade levels of their ***craft.***

We Natsarim are not here to destroy reputations, we tear-down strongholds of false reasoning. We are known by, and show, the fruits of Yahusha. He is wanting to share Truth through us, so mankind will be set free from the traditions and teachings of men. Yahuah's four-lettered Name was *replaced* by translators with **Aduni** (Hebrew), **Kurios** (Greek), **Dominus** (Latin), and **LORD** (Anglican Catholic English). All of these replacements point directly to **BEL** (Baal) if used as proper nouns. They violate the 1st, 2nd, and 3rd Commandments. **Bel** is Nimrod, the first human to become a mighty one, and worshipped as the Sun. *Santa is Nimrod.*

We have inherited nothing but lies and futility, but now we are able to **Google: YAHUSHA** and get to the Truth and call on the only Name given among men by which we must be delivered. (Acts 4:12)
www.fossilizedcustoms.com/yahusha.html

Who Are You, And Why Are You Here?

We all need to be fed (by Yahusha's Ruach) to fulfill His purpose, and finding others who are dead so He can share His life with them as He has done with us.

Yahuah's purposes for us are for our good.

YirmeYahu 29:11 assures us of that fact. No shipwreck is too big for Yahusha. He rescued many people by sending Yusef (Joseph) into Egypt as a slave. Consider Shaul. Yahusha turned this **persecutor of His Name** into one of us, and we know him as our beloved brother now:

"And when we had fallen to the ground, I heard a voice speaking to me, and saying in the Hebrew language, 'Shaul,

Shaul, why do you persecute Me? It is hard for you to kick against the prods.' And I said, *'Who are You, Master?'* And He said, 'I am Yahusha, Whom you persecute. But rise up, and stand on your feet, for I have appeared to you for this purpose, to appoint you a servant and a witness both of what you saw and of those which I shall reveal to you, delivering you from the people, and the gentiles, to whom I now send you, to open their eyes, to turn them from darkness to light, and the authority of satan to Alahim, in order for them to receive forgiveness of sins and an inheritance among those who are set-apart by belief in Me.'" Acts 26:14-18

"And we know that all things work together for good to those who love Alahim, to those called according to His purpose." Romans 8:28

"For the Scripture says to Farah (Greek: Pharaoh), 'For this same purpose I have raised you up, to show My power in you, and that My Name be declared in all the arets." Romans 9:17

Are You Lured By Deceiving Spirits?

A recent comment attracted my attention . . .
Someone said they were searching for their **purpose**, and wanted advice on how to discover it. *Deceiving spirits* lure us away from our purpose for being here, leading the blind into deeper levels of darkness. They desire to have us serve *their* purposes, while promoting *self-empowerment* by opening our minds to the *light* within **us**. Our minds without Yahusha guiding us are darkened, and very easily deceived. Unless we have the Spirit of Yahusha dwelling in us, we do not belong to Him. To discern or test the spirits, look at their fruits in those who are luring you to follow them. The fallen spirits are intensely seductive, and know your weaknesses. They prey on those who are ignorant of Yahuah's Word. Scrying, tarot cards, flying, consulting mediums, talking to the dead (necromancy), serving the host of heaven, palmistry, bowing to images, astrology, and all rebellion lead to death, not life. If you seek your purpose, guard the Commands of Yahuah, keep knocking, and it will be opened to you.
Draw near to Yahuah, and He will draw near to you; Seek His will for you, and you will find it, and inherit everlasting life.
www.fossilizedcustoms.com/purpose.html

QUEEN OF HEAVEN'S
YIRMEYAHU 7
BIRTHDAY ASTRO-BABEL
TORAH INSTITUTE

How To Recognize Idolatry

When families do what the merchants are promoting, they are practicing Babel's fertility culture handed-down to them.
When Yahusha awakens us, and we tell them what is really happening, our families don't share the same perspective.
The wreaths, trees, rabbits, eggs, steeples, domes, cakes and candles, coned hats, astrology signs, calling the 7 weekdays by the names of pagan deities, prayer circles, repetitive prayers, reformatted pagan festivals like Eostre / Easter, Christmas, Valentine's / Lupercalia, Sun-day, Halloween, Olympic games torches to light Zeus cauldrons, etc., are not the way to show our Creator we are His called, chosen people walking as Yahusha walked. Our teachers have led us into confusion, lies, futility, and only arrogant nonsense. The whole world is deceived.
Adopting ancient practices handed-down to us after they became camouflaged under the crust of new ideas has cause the whole of mankind to become drunk from the golden cup of Babel. We can turn a blind eye to it all by saying, *"it doesn't mean that to me,"* or we can choose to stop following the practices.
Idolatry is mankind's most prominent activity, and it drives the world's economy by a yearly cycle of fertility festivals. They are not readily perceived because they are in disguise, hiding in plain sight. The Olympic games mimic the ancient worship of Zeus, whose image is prominently displayed in the central lobby of the United

Nations building in New York City. Another book, **_Strong Delusion_**, will help show far more about what's happened, and why.

NO WITCHCRAFT

Animal House

Rebellion is as the sin of witchcraft. Why do they want to re-build a Temple to house an ark that is not there? The presence of Yahuah departed when they put the zoo animals representing the host of heaven all around the insides, and then put the same images in the mosaics decorating their local synagogues. Some Natsarim teachers are using the zodiac to teach Yahusha's redemption plan today. Yahuah has warned us not to mix or serve Him in the ways of the heathen. Yekezqal 8:9-10: "And he said to me, 'Go in and see the wicked and detestable things they are doing here.' So I went in and looked, and I saw portrayed all over the walls all kinds of crawling things and unclean animals and all the idols of Yisharal." The Sanhedrin (70 rulers) stood up and screamed at Stephen when he spoke in the Name of Yahuah, telling them about their worship of the host of heaven at Acts 7:42.

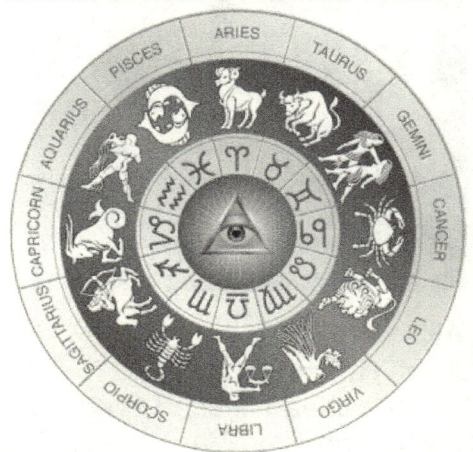

Serving The Host Of Heaven?

The source of all sorcery is Astrology, the great harlot's seduction to an idea of finding **love**, and our perfect match in another person. This **imaginary system of Babylonian Divination** is Astrological sorcery, and we are warned of it in the 1st & 2nd Commandments. Stephen (Acts 7:42) warns of the worship of the **host of heaven**, and the mosaics on the walls and floors of synagogues depict this abominable practice of zoo / zodiac animals.

Yekezqal / Ezekiel chapter 8 describes these living animals shapes being drawn inside the walls of Yahuah's mishkan, driving Him out of the place. The elect are being drawn away into deception of all kinds, and this teaching about Yahuah's redemption plan being written in star patterns on a *heavenly scroll* is a major part of it.

The **redemption plan** is written in the Scripture of Truth, the **festivals of Yahuah** given at Dt. 16 & Uyiqara / Lev. 23.
www.fossilizedcustoms.com/redemption.html

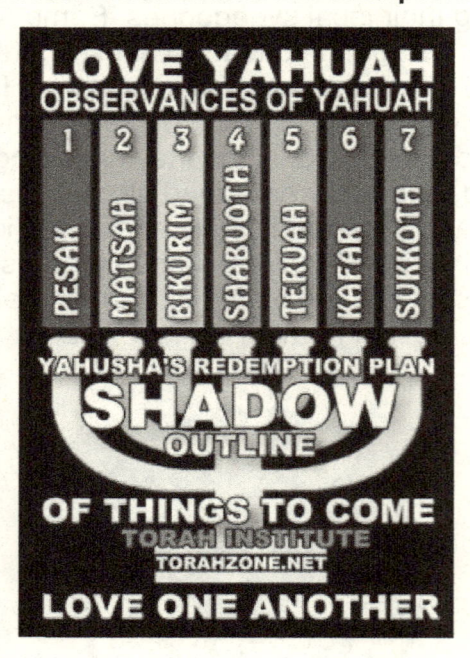

REDEMPTION PLAN

What do the festivals of Yahuah mean?
The Redemption Plan of Yahuah is shadowed in festivals during the year. These show us "the way" Yahusha is redeeming His bride. They are found at Lev. 23 & Dt. 16.
One of them is Yom Kafar, Judgment Day.

Yahusha Himself, and Peter and Paul, reveal the Day of Judgment (by fire) that is still ahead of us. (See book **REAPERS**) The book of Revelation begins with the statement,
"I was in the Spirit on the Master's (kuriakos) **Day."**
This should say **"on Yahuah's Day."** Translators replaced the Name. This was written so we would eventually understand the past, present, and future things; and it continues to say it is to be sent to the assemblies. It is only confusing because our slumbering teachers fumble with the meaning of words in their context.
By not feeding the sheep "every Word that proceeds from the mouth of Yahuah," the sheep remain unprepared for the day set by Yahuah to remove the weeds (Acts 17:30-31).

![REAPERS - TORAH INSTITUTE]

HE HAS SET A DAY
"Truly, then, having overlooked these times of ignorance, Alahim now commands all men everywhere to repent because He has set a day on which He is going to judge the world in righteousness by a Man whom He has appointed, having given proof of this to all by raising Him from the dead."
Acts 17:30-31

A DAY IS DESCRIBED AT YUAL (Joel) **2**
A DAY OF EVIL (PROVERBS 16:4)
A DAY OF DARKNESS (YUAL 2:2)
A DAY OF BURNING (MALAKI 4:1)
A DAY FOR REAPING THE WEEDS (MT. 24:28)
THE EAGLES ARE THE REAPERS ON A FUTURE YOM KAFAR AND IT CONCERNS THE FALL APPOINTED TIMES
ACTS 27:9, LEV 23:27

Are Codes Real, Or Misdirection?
What Scripture verse informs us to follow leaders that have uncovered newly discovered **codes**? The **real message** they no longer remember. Misdirection is all people hear from pastors. The more complicated and mysterious their ideas sound, the more people follow them. The simple believe every word, but the clever

ones watch their step. **"To the Torah and to the Witness! If they do not speak according the this Word, it is because they have no daybreak!"** YashaYahu (Is.) 8:20

YirmeYahu (Jer.) 23:29-40:
"'Is not My Word like a fire?' declares Yahuah, 'and like a hammer that shatters a rock?
Therefore see, I am against the prophets,' declares Yahuah, 'who steal My Words every one from his neighbor.
See, I am against the prophets,' declares Yahuah, 'who use their tongues and say, "He declares."
See, I am against those who prophesy false dreams,' declares Yahuah, 'and relate them, and lead My people astray by their falsehoods and by their reckless boasting. But I Myself did not send them nor have I commanded them. And they do not profit this people at all,' declares Yahuah.
'And when these people or the prophet or the priest ask you, saying, "What is the message of Yahuah?" then you shall say to them, "What message?" I shall forsake you,' declares Yahuah. 'As for the prophet and the priest and the people who say, "The message of Yahuah," I shall punish that man and his house. This is what each one says to his neighbor, and each one to his brother, "What has Yahuah answered?" and, "What has Yahuah spoken?"
But the message of Yahuah you no longer remember!
For every man's message is his own word, for you have changed the Words of the living Alahim, Yahuah Tsabaoth, our Alahim! This is what you say to the prophet, "What has Yahuah answered you?" and, "What has Yahuah spoken?"
But since you say, "The message of Yahuah!" therefore thus said Yahuah, "Because you say this word, 'The message of Yahuah,' and I have sent to you, saying, 'Do not say, "The message of Yahuah,"' therefore see, I, I shall utterly forget you and cast you away from My presence, along with the city that I gave you and your fathers. And I shall put an everlasting reproach on you, and an everlasting shame that is not forgotten.' " -YirmeYahu (Jer.) 23:29-40 BYNV

Pictographic Letters Gone Wild!
People are being fed *wormwood* by those who are altering the message of Yahuah's Words.
Teachers are ignoring the root meaning of words and forming out-of-context interpretations, seeking to discover codes and secret layers of meaning. They build-up imagined meanings they find into sentences. Hieroglyphs are now being mixed with Eberith letters to form a chain of letters into sentences. This approach to Scripture by deceiving forces (spirits) is a form of **divination**.

Some use Scriptures as if they are Tarot cards, receiving false impressions through teachers (gurus, rabbis) seeking followers to mislead. **Kabbalah** is full-blown **Gnosticism**, and parallels the mystical thought of Hinduism's *four levels* of interpretation.
www.fossilizedcustoms.com/kabbalah.html

GOT YOKE?
A YOKE IS A TEACHING
CONSIDER THE SOURCE OF EVERYTHING YOU ARE PRACTICING
RELIGIOUS GARB OF PAGANS WHO WORSHIP "FORCES"

HINDU KHATA | CATHOLIC / CHRISTIAN STOLE | RABBINIC KATAN

There's far more deception going on than a fake name. Yahusha's yoke is light, and thankfully has no Christmas, Sunday morning assemblies, Lent, or paying people to tell you obedience sickens them. Disobedience is lawlessness, and 1 Yn. 3:4 calls it sin.
The dragon is enraged at those who obey the Commandments of Alahim, and hold to the testimony of Yahusha (Rev. 12:17).
Love one another, and determine the tree by evaluating the fruit you see it bearing. Yahusha bears good fruit in those He indwells.
Yahusha is the way, the Truth, and the life.

Those who will not receive a love for the Truth will be sent a strong delusion.

www.fossilizedcustoms.com/strongdelusion.html

Holy water, hailing Krishna, and praying with Shiva beads won't fix what's about to unleash. Yahusha is coming sooner than anyone expects, but people are still dreaming soundly. If we fail to train children properly, we will raise up lawless generations that will bring about destruction. If we allow idolatry, Yahuah Himself will bring the destruction. Look how He feels about teaching little children to do the wrong thing:
 "And whoever causes one of these little ones who believe in Me to stumble, it is better for him if a millstone were hung around his neck, and he were thrown into the sea." - Mark 9:42

LOVE TRAINING

The greatest harm comes from keeping children from learning how to love. The **Ten Commandments are the training** which both our moral leadership and government leadership have intentionally shunned. The results are being reaped, and teachers are cowering in fear, and police are overwhelmed. Single-moms and single dads are raising generation after generation of lawless, spiteful children. The world is filled with lawlessness, and love is growing cold.

Who is to blame? The ones Yahuah blames are the teachers who **tell you to disobey** the most wonderful gift humanity has ever been given, besides Yahusha's redemptive blood. (YashaYahu 9:16)

These are more precious than any treasure

Post them on all your doorposts and on your gates

COVENANT OF LOVE

1
I AM YAHUAH YOUR ALAHIM
HAVE NO OTHER BEFORE MY FACE

2
YOU DO NOT BOW TO IMAGES

3
YOU DO NOT CAST THE NAME OF
YAHUAH YOUR ALAHIM TO RUIN

4
REMEMBER SHABATH
GUARD IT AS QODESH

5
RESPECT YOUR FATHER & MOTHER

6
YOU DO NOT MURDER

7
YOU DO NOT BREAK WEDLOCK

8
YOU DO NOT STEAL

9
YOU DO NOT BEAR A MALICIOUS
WITNESS AGAINST YOUR NEIGHBOR

10
YOU DO NOT COVET YOUR
NEIGHBOR'S WIFE, HOUSE, FIELD,
SERVANTS, ANIMALS, OR ANYTHING
BELONGING TO YOUR NEIGHBOR

ヨYヨZ

I AM YAHUAH, THAT IS MY NAME
LOVE ME AND GUARD MY COMMANDS
LOVE YOUR NEIGHBOR AS YOURSELF
LOVE ONE ANOTHER AS I HAVE LOVED YOU

TORAHZONE.NET   LAMBLEGACYFOUNDATION.COM   NATSARIMSEARCH.COM
BE MORE THAN A BELIEVER, BE A A DOER OF THE WORD
BECOME ONE OF THE NATSARIM - BRANCHES OF YAHUSHA

DO YOU SEE ANYTHING IMPOSSIBLE TO OBEY?
WRITE THEM ON YOUR DOORPOSTS & GATES
TEACH THEM TO YOUR CHILDREN & GRANDCHILDREN
THIS IS THE WAY, WALK IN IT

Sunday: Yahusha gave no such instruction?

22 years after Yahusha ascended, Shabath is still mentioned in Acts: 1:12, 13:14, 13:42, 13:43, 16:13, 17:1, 17:2 (mentions 3 consecutive Shabaths), and 18:4.

FACT: There is no instruction for anyone to observe Sunday in the Scripture of Truth *anywhere*.

Today, some of the **leading Baptists** have admitted that the Sunday Shabath isn't in the scriptures as Dr. Edward Hiscox states: *"There was and is a commandment to keep holy the Sabbath day, but that Sabbath day was not on Sunday...It will be said, however, and with some show of triumph, that the Sabbath was transferred from the seventh to the first day of the week....where can the record of such a transaction be found? Not in the New Testament.*
Of course, I quite well know that Sunday did come into use in early Christian history as a religious day, as we learn from the Christian Fathers and other sources. But what a pity that it comes branded with the mark of paganism, and christened with the name of a sun god, when adopted and sanctioned by the papal apostasy, and bequeathed as a sacred legacy to Protestantism!"
[Dr. Edward Hiscox, author of The Baptist Manual]

Natsarim are not arrogant; we are aware of what's coming. Shabath is the sign of the everlasting Covenant, the 7th day of each week when we do not buy and sell, but stay in our place to rest. Those who allow themselves to buy and sell have another mark of authority (Rome's), a teaching authority I used to obey until I joined with Yahusha. Because I love Him, I obey Him. He forgave me for ignoring Him for years and doing as I pleased. A man is the servant of the one he obeys (Romans 6:16), and there is only one reason I love the Commandments; Yahusha changed my heart. If ha shatan (BEL-ZEBUB, *LORD of FLIES*) is now teaching people to obey Yahuah's everlasting Covenant, such an idea conflicts with Revelation 12:17. Prophecies yet-to-be-fulfilled prove the Shabath will continue during the tribulation, return of Yahusha, and beyond: Mt. 24:20 (pray your flight will not be on Shabath); YashaYahu / Is. 56:2-5, 66:23; and the festival of Sukkoth at Yahusha's return, Zechariah 14:17. Paul warned us all at 2 Timothy 4:2-4 how men would turn away from Truth and teach **myths**. Paul's charge to Timothy: ***Preach the Word!***

Beware The Jabberwock My Son! (confused speech)

The teachers have fallen far from the Truth, and are under the spell of confused languages. They have been given great authority by the dragon (king of Babel), and produce bad fruit.
Research the Hebrew Name YAHUSHA. This was avoided by translators who substituted it with IESV, a christogram standing in place of it. A christogram is an encryption that stands in place of the proper name of a deity. Using nonsense terms for concealing one's deity was practiced by mystagogues as far back as the 70-year captivity at Babel. Examples are IESV, IC-XC, IHS, LORD, and JABULON used by the upper degrees of Templar masonry's pursuit of G (Gnosticism, ancient knowledge). The planners are globalists, going by many names like Jesuit Illuminati, the NWO. The dragon is enraged at the woman (Yahusha's bride), and makes war against her offspring (Natsarim, branches), who obey the Turah and testify of Yahusha (Rev. 12:17). We overcome by the blood of Yahusha, Who comes in the Name of Yahuah.

www.fossilizedcustoms.com/yahusha.html

Speaking Truth causes the false teaching authority (behemoth, beast) to roar in pain. Those who dig into the original Eberith (Hebrew) language and script find themselves perplexed at the gross ignorance on exhibit throughout the world. Does no one care that they have been deceived to call on a nonsense word, JESUS, that is an utterly impossible word to have existed in the time of our Deliverer's walk on this Earth?
Here's the first page of an article from the Ambassador's Package:

JABBERWOCK
HOW TO IDENTIFY THE BEHEMOTH

Beware The Jabberwock My Son
(teachers promoting confused speech)
The teachers have fallen far from the Truth, preferring to speak in confused languages. They have been given great authority by the dragon (king of Babel), and produce bad fruit. Research the Hebrew Name YAHUSHA. It was avoided by translators who substituted it with **IESV**, a Christogram, a device used to encrypt the proper name of a deity. Using nonsense terms for concealing one's deity was practiced by mystagogues as far back as the 70-year captivity at Babel. Examples are **IESV, IC-XC, IHS, LORD**, and JABULON used by the upper degrees of Templar masonry's pursuit of **G** (Gnosticism). The planners are a consortium of titled globalists and controllers, such as the Jesuit-Illuminati, or UN.

JABBERWOCK
CONFUSED SPEECH

A **behemoth** (beast) has been given great authority by the dragon, who is enraged at the woman (Yahusha's bride), and makes war against her offspring (Natsarim, branches), who obey Torah and testify of Yahusha (Rev. 12:17). We overcome by the blood of Yahusha, Who comes in the Name of **Yahuah**. Yahusha will end the behemoth's reign of terror.

SPEAK TRUTH, AND THE BEHEMOTH ROARS IN PAIN

The 4th beast is a composite of one huge authoritarian regime. Danial and Revelation align with Yahusha's perspective of how we can identify the rebellion against His instructions in the world around us. The rebellion of Nimrod, and the very first organized crime he set up at the tower, has grown into a worldwide behemoth of idolatry. Babel, Medo-Persian, Greece, and Rome have all managed to focus on the manipulation of forces (such as the host of heaven) to serve mankind, not Yahuah. If we speak Truth, and call on the one Name given among men by which we must be delivered, Yahusha, those programmed by the behemoth's teaching authority will roar against us. Those given orders (ordained) to teach by the authority of their part in the behemoth must stay within the boundaries, or their overseers will disfellowship them. Only the teachings permitted by men are allowed, being tightly controlled by the religious thugs within their group or sub-culture. As people pour their wealth and physical strength into what they believe is pleasing to their overseers (turn page)

JABBERWOCK is named after a poem many have taken to be nonsense, but yet ingeniously designed to contain imagery of Babel. At age 39, Charles Lutwidge Dodgson (pen name, *Louis Carroll*) wrote his sequel to *Alice's Adventures In Wonderland*, titling it *Through The Looking Glass*. It contains the familiar poems *Humpty Dumpty*, and *The Jabberwock* - a *play-on-words* meaning *confusion*, with the Welsh term Wock, for talk. The confusion of our speech originates at Babel, yet our teachers seem to be unwilling to be restored to a pure lip and desire to remain in the same pigsty they were brought up in. As repentant children, some want to return to their Father's household, recalling how far they have fallen from their original love. Humpty Dumpty is a metaphor for the Truth, trusted and seen as a fragile Eggman sitting on a high wall.
Once what was believed to be Truth is exposed to be a lie, its power over all who trusted in it is shattered beyond repair. Men's traditions are the patterns of Babel, and only conform to the patterns of the world. When Babel falls, the king of Babel (dragon) will suffer the same consequences as *Humpty Dumpty*.
Truth matters, and so do the words we are sent to speak. If a tune is played with missing or incorrect notes, how will the tune be recognized by the indistinct sounds? (1 Korinthians 14:8)
Yahusha's Name, culture, speech, and Turah are all rejected by most teachers claiming to know Him. Revising everything to fit the pattern (philosophies) of the world is what we are told not to do by Yahuah (Dt. 18, Dt. 30, YirmeYahu 10:2-4, Kolossians 2:8).
The opposite of that has occurred, and mankind has become a prey of human traditions to the extent of becoming **xenophobic** toward Yahusha's Name, culture, speech, and Turah. We, His Natsarim, are here to prepare the way for His return.
Those who claim to know Him love all He has redeemed. If we do not, we lie, and the Truth is not in us.

Racism And Bigotry
Everyone alive today are descended from Noak, and Shem, Kam, and Yafeth born to him by his wife NaAmah. Yahuah created all the nationalities from one blood (Acts 17:26). Yahusha is most likely dark genetically, being descended from Eber, however He looks on the heart, being the Creator of all things seen, and unseen. Paul warned us not to involve in quarrels or debates about genealogies

(Titus 3:9), and Yahusha warned us it would be a sign of His coming when we would become divided over it (Mt. 24:7).
www.fossilizedcustoms.com/mirror.html

YirmeYahu saw the destruction of Yerushalom in 586 BCE.
He had prophesied of its destruction, but no one would listen. YirmeYahu (Jeremiah) wrote of the last days at chapter 16 verse 19. What do you think he was talking about when he mentioned the lies and falsehood (delusions, errors) passed down to the gentiles from their fathers? His own people imprisoned him for telling the Truth, and the Babylonians set him free. The crowds are confused because their teachers lead them into error and disobedience.
Is it mentally healthy to tell children to believe fantasies about tooth fairies, Santa, hunting for eggs hidden in rabbit holes to honor Diana (Ishtar / Eastre), dressing up as goblins to trick goblins, talking to dead relatives (necromancy), or believing the host of heaven are aligning with a zoo of animals that determine their future? Is it rational to expect good results in them later on as adults? By sowing seeds of delusion in little minds, the whole world has become mad, and the Day of Yahuah is drawing very close.
http://fossilizedcustoms.com/strongdelusion.html

Were You Raised To Believe In Santa?
The prophets remind us repeatedly to obey the Commandments, and teach them diligently to our children, and never let them depart from our lips. The whole world has gone mad, having become drunk on the teachings of Babel. The Living Word appeared among us as the Son of Adam, and everything He did and said supported the prophets He inspired to write about Himself, and how the Word would become trodden underfoot by men, replaced by traditions. For many generations, witchcraft has been taken into the bosoms of children by way of their parents' traditions. From that perspective, the prophecy at YirmeYahu 16:19 is unfolding more and more as people are learning the Truth. The same prophet mentions a great deliverance at chapter 31, and verse 6 mentions us, His Natsarim. The King of Babel is led by the dragon. Santa is Nimrod; the first Sun deity, promoted at the birthday of the Sun, the winter solstice.

www.fossilizedcustoms.com/christmas.html

> **NIMROD'S SECRET IDENTITY**
> YASHAYAHU 14 13-14
>
> LET ME GO UP TO THE SHAMAYIM,
> LET ME RAISE MY THRONE ABOVE THE STARS OF AL
> LET ME SIT IN THE MOUNT OF MEETING
> **ON THE SIDES OF THE NORTH**
> LET ME GO ABOVE THE HEIGHTS OF THE CLOUDS
> **LET ME BE LIKE THE MOST HIGH**
> KING OF BABEL

It's Like They're Hypnotized

The Christian pastors know, but those who listen to them don't immediately perceive they are following nothing Yahusha wants them to, *while doing everything He warned us **not** to do*. They are unaware they are following one fertility festival after the other, ... after the other, ... in a drunken fantasy cycle whose provenance is not the Word of Yahuah, but rather Babel (confusion).

Making every thought obedient to Turah is easy and only possible if one belongs to Yahusha (see 1 Yn. 2:4).

Hallel u Yah: *you praise Yah*

Many pastors are learning that **Yahusha** is found 216 times in the TaNaK, and was first used in the text at Numbers 13:16 when Mushah added one letter to Husha the son of Nun (hay-uau-shin-ayin). The original Eberith (Hebrew) spelling of Yahusha is found in the 5 letters **yod-hay-uau-shin-ayin**, easily found by looking at the *interlinear text* at Zechariah (ZekarYah) chapter 3. Miryam and Yusef never called Yahusha *"Jesus."*

James Strong's Concordance of the KJV was published in 1890, and carried forward a few impossible letters (such as J and W) and niqqud marks (from the 8th century).

The person known as Joshua, and our Mashiak Yahusha, have the same Hebrew spelling yod-hay-uau-shin-ayin. The modern letter "double-U" is a doubling of the Latin letter shaped V, invented by a type-setter around 1450 CE. There are no letters J or W in Eberith, however they are part of the process in purging the leaven.

The phonology is derived from the Eberith script, and our Greco-Latin letters often get in the way, or fail us in our attempt to purify our lips. **www.fossilizedcustoms.com/w.html**

What Was The Old Covenant?
Did Yahusha annul the Ten Commandments, or rather did He annul the former priesthood that offered animal blood for atonement?
A huge misunderstanding surrounds the meaning of the word LAW as taught by the circus. The word TURAH means instruction.
The everlasting Covenant of love was INSIDE the ark written in stone, now written on our hearts by Yahusha, if we receive Him and turn away from sin. Sin is lawlessness (1 Yn. 3:4). Our love for obeying the Ten Words is powered by His indwelling. The law that changed was performed by the obsolete priesthood (Hebrews 8:13) and their offerings of animal blood, written on a SCROLL and placed BESIDE the ark (Dt. 31:26). It was imperfect because it could not redeem, nor instill a desire to be obedient. This change in the law required a change in the priesthood. Animal blood offered for sin through the old priesthood merely pointed to the one-time offering of Yahusha's blood, which now has redeemed us completely. The old covenant was written on a scroll, but the renewed Covenant is cut in our hearts by Yahusha, sprinkling our hearts with His precious blood. By trusting in His blood to cover our sins, we now have His Spirit which confirms that we have complete redemption from sin. We no longer have the former desire to sin because He shares His Mind with us, and feel how it makes Him feel if we disobey. We know Him if we obey His Commandments, and His Spirit dwell in us. Anyone who does not have His Spirit dwelling in them does not know Him, nor do they belong to Him.
(1 Yn. 2:4, Romans 8:9)   **www.fossilizedcustoms.com/lie.html**

Do You Love The Ten Commandments Yet?
Pursue your zone of purpose, the reason for which you were created. My own discovery of that purpose was an awakening. When we awaken, the delusions we were involved in from our childhood clear away like a fog dispersing. We have to turn around, and stop resisting the Creator's will, and just do it.
It is never about what we desire, but rather to learn to cooperate with the Creator and His purpose. Doing things His way always

works for the good of everyone. We were designed to perform (live in, abide in) the Commandments.
They are easy, perfect, and everlasting (See Psalm 119, Ecclesiastes 12:13-14). Receive a love of the Truth, or be sent a strong delusion to believe the lie.

When Accused Of Being A False Teacher
Our enemy is not flesh and blood. The enemy rules the minds of those who are weak in the Word of Yahuah, easily controllable by false reasoning (strongholds). The best place to begin is sow the Word into your mind, and use it as a sword when under attack. One of my favorite things to do is share the Ten Commandments with someone I've just met, so they know who they are dealing with. When under direct attack, our enemy will flee when we use the Word. Consider the pain these words might cause a demonic spirit:
"Let the words of my mouth, and the meditation in my heart, be pleasing before you, Yahuah, my Rock and my Redeemer!" Ps. 19:14
Our lips are altars, and He inhabits the praises of Yisharal.
We Natsarim are engaged in a war as soldiers, and everyone will know we are Yahusha's disciples (talmidim) if we have love for one another.
I was trained by Jesuits, but I was never one of them. Their maxims were exercises to program young minds, but it did not work on me. Yahusha knows our motives, but He replaces those with what He desires (giving us the desires of our hearts). Whoever has been given the desire to destroy the reputation of another, it is most likely not Yahusha. The best advice is to always consult Him before acting on what to do. He controls our thoughts if we hold them captive to His will, not our own will. By our words we will be declared upright, and by our words we will be condemned. We must never condemn one another, for we are not our own, having been bought with a price (His blood). Who are we to judge a servant that is not ours?
(see Romans 14 and full context)

Confusion Of The Nations
Nimrod's rebellion (Babel) is prevalent world-wide, and settlements of Yisharal's sea empire left many way-marks. Some of the members of the large expeditions from the ports at Tyre and Sidon were BEL / Baal worshipers. Yahuah warned His people to not learn the ways of the heathen, nor serve Him in their way. That ship has long-since

sailed, and Danial 12 explains that in the last days the wise will lead many to right-ruling and made spotless and refined, however the wicked will continue to be wicked because they were lied to by the beast and the false prophet.

Old Covenant vs. Renewed Covenant

The law of sin and death involved the old covenant placed beside the ark (Dt. 31:26), explained to be the old priesthood's prescriptions for temporary atonement by the now-defunct Aharonic priesthood (Hebrews 8:13). Animal blood redeemed no one. The renewed Melkizedek priesthood now in effect forever redeems us completely by the perfect offering of Yahusha's blood. The Ten Commandments stand forever, as the everlasting Covenant. The confusion between these two has caused the circus to believe they can throw out the Ten Commandments, but this is the lie that even the elect may be tempted to fall for. Reading further will show you the perspective of a Fifth Estate which is beyond the control of the World Order.

The Fifth Estate exposes them all. The World Order of Nimrod continues within the 3 estates, headed by Nimrod's vicar (office of the papacy ruling vicariously in Nimrod's place). A fourth estate known as the media blossomed with the printing press (1450 CE). A fifth estate exposes the other 4, which is the point of view you are now seeing. I expose the Societas IESV in many books, articles, and videos, but I do not judge the people seduced by the seducing spirits, some may wake up later after meeting the risen Yahusha, as our beloved brother Paul did on the road to Damascus.

www.fossilizedcustoms.com/agenda.html

Who Are The Jesuits?

A military organism posing as a religious institution, Societas IESV is the term in Latin. We often recognize these dissemblers by the initials S.J. after their name.

Inigo de Loyola founded the *Societas IESV* in August 1534 as a military order to combat the effects of the Reformation, and **restore the papacy to world domination** (all secular power on Earth). This remains the **agenda** as expressed in the Jesuit Oath.

See: **www.fossilizedcustoms.com/jesuitoath.htm**

The Magisterium's official name for the Jesuit Order is **Regimini militantis ecclesiae,** a Latin phrase meaning:
"To the government of the church militant."
Their brain-washing doesn't work on everyone, and I'm proof.
While under the control of the Jesuits teaching me as a child, the **World Order** was explained to me as the teaching authority I was compelled to obey, and adhere to for the rest of eternity. Now it sounds like the principalities in the spiritual realm causing the world to remain confused, and rebelling against the will of Yahuah.
As a little child I heard them say the authority of the world is arranged in this order: God, Pope, priesthood, government (state), parents. Within this we find the ancient World Order of three estates, CLERGY, NOBILITY, and LAITY (the common folk). This is the pattern of control set in place by the enemy of Yahuah, Satan. The whole package of lies is held together like a steel frameword with no rivets. They sell the lie that receive sacraments is the path to salvation, and burning in a non-existant place called Purgatory will burn away whatever the sacraments didn't take care of. They hold to the idea they have their authority to rule the whole world because of the false teaching called **apostolic succession**.

We've all heard it said that Satan is the **god** of this world. I heard and saw things that were outrageous to my mind, and asking questions only made them angry and even more suspicious to me. I shut up and kept my head down. The things they taught us to do were abominations: praying to dead people, kneeling in front of images and praying to them (demons), signing with hand gestures, touching what they called holy water, and the day called Sun-day, on which we went to a steeple/pillar where we all pretended whoever it was we were worshipping with that behavior was watching all of us, and very pleased. I later learned all of these are inherited from Hinduism. An innocent child cannot be held responsible for being led into such idolatry, but those who continue after hearing the Truth will become responsible if they continue with it, and if they do not warn others.
Every department of Nazi Germany under Hitler was headed by a Jesuit. The pope of that time was known as "Hitler's Pope."
You might want to Google this to confirm what I'm saying.
Natsarim were called **Huguenots** in the Jesuit Oath cited next.

Hitler greets two Roman Catholic officials in 1934. Hitler said: "As for the Jews, I am just carrying on with the same policy which the Catholic Church has adopted for fifteen hundred years..."

The Jesuits Oath:

I, *A.B.* , now in the presence of Almighty God, the blessed Virgin Mary, the blessed Michael the archangel, the blessed St. John Baptist, the holy apostles St. Peter and St. Paul, and the saints and sacred hosts of heaven, and to you my ghostly father, do declare from my heart, without mental reservation, that his holiness Pope Urban is Christ's vicar general, and is the true and only head of the Catholic or universal church throughout the earth; and that by the virtue of the keys of binding and loosing given to his holiness by my Saviour Jesus Christ, he hath power to depose heretical kings, princes, states, commonwealths, and governments, all being illegal, without his sacred confirmation, and that they may safely be destroyed; therefore, to the utmost of my power I shall and will defend this doctrine, and his holiness's rights and customs against all usurpers of the heretical (or Protestant) authority whatsoever; especially against the now pretended authority and Church of England, and all adherents, in regard that they and she be usurpal and heretical, opposing the sacred mother Church of Rome. I do renounce and disown any allegiance as due to any heretical king, prince, or state, named Protestants, or obedience to any of their inferior magistrates or officers.
I do further declare, that the doctrine of the Church of England, of the Calvinists, Huguenots, and of other of the name

Protestants, to be damnable, and they themselves are damned, and to be damned, that will not forsake the same. I do further declare, that I will help, assist, and advise all, or any of his holiness's agents in any place, wherever I shall be, in England, Scotland, and Ireland, or in any other territory or kingdom I shall come to; to do my utmost to extirpate the heretical Protestants' doctrine, and to destroy all their pretended powers, regal or otherwise.

I do further promise and declare, that notwithstanding I am dispensed with to assume any religion heretical for the propagating of the mother church's interest, to keep secret and private all her agents' counsels from time to time, as they intrust me, and not to divulge, directly or indirectly, by word, writing, or circumstances whatsoever; but to execute all that shall be proposed, given in charge, or discovered into me, by you my ghostly father, or by any of this sacred convent.

All which I, A. B., do swear by the blessed Trinity, and blessed sacrament, which I now am to receive, to perform, and on my part to keep inviolably; And do call all the heavenly and glorious host of heaven to witness these my real intentions to keep this my oath. In testimony hereof, I take this most holy and blessed sacrament of the eucharist; and witness the same further with my hand and seal in the face of this holy convent, this ----- day of ----- An. Dom., & c., McGavins Protestant, Vol. ii. p. 256.

The Jesuit Extreme Oath of Induction as recorded in the Congressional Record of the U.S.A. (House Bill 1523, Contested election case of Eugene C. Bonniwell, against Thos. S. Butler, Feb. 15, 1913, pp. 3215-3216):

Jesuit Extreme Oath of Induction

I _____, now in the presence of Almighty God, the Blessed Virgin Mary, the Blessed Michael the Archangel, the Blessed St. John the Baptist, the Holy Apostles, Peter and Paul, and all the Saints, sacred hosts of Heaven, and to you, my ghostly Father, the Superior General of the Society of Jesus, founded by St. Ignatius Loyola, in the Pontification of Paul the Third, and continued to the present, do by the womb of the virgin, the matrix of God, and the rod of Jesus Christ, declare and swear that his holiness, the Pope, is Christ's Vice-regent, and is the true and only head of the Catholic or Universal Church throughout the earth; and that by the virtue of the keys of binding and loosing, given to his Holiness by my Savior, Jesus Christ, he hath power to depose heretical kings, princes, states, commonwealths and governments, all being illegal without his sacred confirmation, and that they may be safely destroyed.

I do further declare, that I will help and assist and advise all or any of his Holiness' agents in any place wherever I shall be, and do my utmost to extirpate the heretical Protestant or Liberal doctrines and to destroy all their pretended powers, legal or otherwise.

I do further promise and declare, that notwithstanding I am dispensed with to assume any religion heretical, for the propagating of the Mother Church's interest, to keep secret and private all her agents' counsels, from time to time as they may instruct me, and not to divulge directly or indirectly, by word, writing, or circumstances whatever; but to execute all that shall be proposed given in charge or discovered unto me, by you, my ghostly father. ...

I do further promise and declare, that I will have no opinion or will of my own, or any mental reservation whatever, even as a corpse or cadaver but unhesitatingly obey each and every command that I may receive from my superiors in the Militia of the Pope and Jesus Christ.

That I will go to any part of the world, whatsoever, without murmuring and will be submissive in all things whatsoever communicated to me. ... I do further promise and declare, that I will, when opportunity presents, make and wage relentless war, secretly or openly, against all heretics, Protestants and Liberals, as I am directed to do to extirpate and exterminate them from the face of the whole earth, and that I will spare neither sex, age nor condition, and that I will hang, waste, boil, flay, strangle and bury alive these infamous heretics; rip up the stomachs and wombs of their women and crush their infants heads against the wall, in order to annihilate forever their execrable race.

That when the same cannot be done openly, I will secretly use the poison cup, the strangulation cord, the steel of the

poniard, or the leaden bullet, regardless of the honor, rank, dignity or authority of the person or persons whatsoever may be their condition in life, either public or private, as I at any time may be directed so to do by any agent of the Pope or superior of the Brotherhood of the Holy Faith of the Society of Jesus.
(These words are essentially the oath of an assassin to his or her master - in this case, the General of the Jesuits)

RACIAL BIGOTRY IN THE WILDERNESS

Mt. 24 tells us just prior to Yahusha coming back, nation will rise up against nation. This word is specific, meaning "nationality," or ethnic group. This fear of other skin coloring has been spreading like gangrene / leprosy all over the Earth. They forget they were all delivered out of Africa, among many other captive peoples, and all were united by Yahuah. Mushah (Moses) married a Cushite, a descendant of Kam (Ham), and Miryam didn't like her skin color. Yahuah struck her with leprosy on the spot . . . Many details about this new bigotry stronghold are covered in a video, found at this webpage: www.fossilizedcustoms.com/mirror.html

Calendar Controversies Are In Abundance

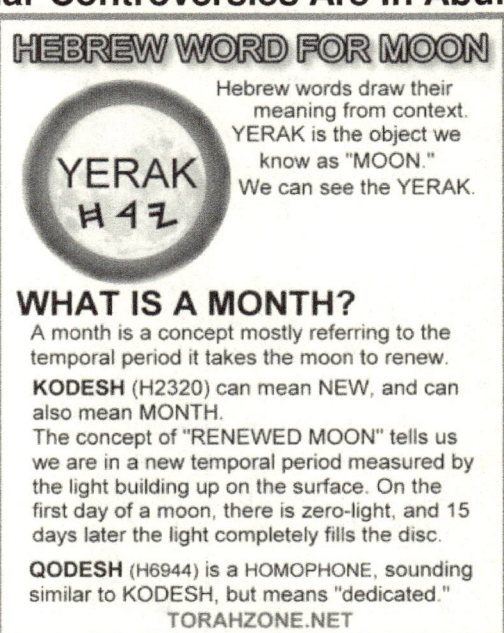

HEBREW WORD FOR MOON

YERAK

Hebrew words draw their meaning from context. YERAK is the object we know as "MOON." We can see the YERAK.

WHAT IS A MONTH?

A month is a concept mostly referring to the temporal period it takes the moon to renew.

KODESH (H2320) can mean NEW, and can also mean MONTH.

The concept of "RENEWED MOON" tells us we are in a new temporal period measured by the light building up on the surface. On the first day of a moon, there is zero-light, and 15 days later the light completely fills the disc.

QODESH (H6944) is a HOMOPHONE, sounding similar to KODESH, but means "dedicated."

TORAHZONE.NET

When does a *new month* period begin?
The major differences we see are based on the starting day for a new month. Many are using the Islamic **sighted crescent**, which was adopted by Anan in Babylon in the year 767. His new sect was called the Karaites. Anan had been arrested by the Islamic Caliph for sedition. While in prison awaiting execution, Anan found a way to avoid death by recognizing the Islamic way of beginning a month. The sighting of a crescent shows the fully-built first day of a new month, however the confusion about the starting point is caused by misunderstanding the difference in the Hebrew words KODESH and YERAK.

Why Many Teachers Use Moon Crescents
The sliver (crescent) of light on the Moon indicates the fully-built first day of the month, and *confirms the second day is now building.* The Islamic method and the Karaite method both use a sighted-Moon crescent. Anan, the founder of the Karaites, adopted the sighted-Moon crescent in the year 767 while he was under arrest for rebellion. The Islamic Caliph in Babylon spared his life after Anan explained this was the basis of his rebellion, and this division between the Orthodox and Karaite sects has persisted to this day. The confusion among our teachers over many things has caused bitterness and raging hatred over petty misunderstandings.
www.fossilizedcustoms.com/sightedmoonorigins.html

Does the Week Re-start Every New Month?
The Lunar-Sabbath ideas began about 1997, and then books and articles spread this new understanding, and there is no agreement among the various subsets of those trying to explain it. The first day of a month is confirmed after it is passed when sighted by and sliver of light seen at sunset. The 7-day week (shabua, "seven") is never related with the month, or aspects of the Moon. The Moon rules the night as the Sun rules the day. Shemoth 40:1-2 is one evidence of many that the first day of that month was not a Shabath. The first day of the 7th month is a rest day, but not necessarily a 7th day of a week. There is no Scripture telling us to re-start counting the days of a week by looking at the Moon; the lack of manna was used to re-train the tribes when the 7th day of a week arrived. The **Moon** is never mentioned to indicate when the first day of a **week** is. In the count from First-fruits to Shabuoth, there are 7 intact weeks, and up

to the morrow after the 7th Shabath, Scripture indicates the sum of 50 days. (Uyiqara / Lev. 23:16) **www.fossilizedcustoms.com/moon.html**

Who Is Ruach Ha Qodesh?

Natsarim are correcting an error today that has been passed down by the teaching authority at Rome. This Magisterium is led by an anti-Mashiak spirit controlling what is taught, and who gets to teach. There was never a person named JESUS (hay-sus) living on Earth 2000 years ago, but rather Yahuah our Creator is Yahusha ha Mashiak, and He alone is the one true Alahim Who inhabited flesh. There is no other to place trust in. Yn. 14 explains who we are to believe in. Acts 20:28-30 tells us the Ruach ha Qodesh "shed His Own blood" for our transgressions against His Turah:

"Therefore take heed to yourselves and to all the flock, among which the Ruach ha Qodesh has made you overseers, to shepherd the assembly of Alahim which He has purchased with His own blood. For I know this, that after my departure savage wolves shall come in among you, not sparing the flock. Also from among yourselves men shall arise, speaking distorted teachings, to draw away the talmidim after themselves." - BYNV

www.fossilizedcustoms.com/omnipresence.html

PILATE'S IDENTIFICATION MARKER ON THE STAKE:
ayaz IS WRITTEN IN ACROSTIC:

ヨYヨZ ソムYヨZヨ ソ⌐ソY Z4トソヨ OWYヨZ

MODERN ENGLISH TRANSLITERATION:
YAHUSHA HANATSARI UMELEK HAYAHUDIM

LATIN TRANSLATION:
IESVSNAZARENVSREXIVDAEORVM

GREEK TRANSLATION:
ΟΥΤΟΣΕΣΤΙΝΟΒΑΣΙΛΕΥΣΤΩΝΙΟΥΔΑΙΩΝ

TORAH INSTITUTE RESEARCH

Baptized Into A Circus?

They drop you backwards as they baptize you in the name Jesus. Find out if that's the real Name of your Redeemer. What does Jesus mean, and in what language? What does Yahusha mean, and in what language? Immersion is when we call on the Name of Yahusha for the forgiveness of our sins, and pledging our

obedience to the Eternal Covenant. It is His blood that covers our sins, and His Name that seals us for the day of our redemption, and He circumcises our hearts to receive a love for the Truth.
I've watched as others entered the water to call on the Name of Yahusha as I did also in a creek one night when Yahusha came on me to do it. We pledge our lives only to Yahusha, Who purchased us with His Own blood, not animal blood. Please read Acts chapters 19 through 20:28.
www.fossilizedcustoms.com/circumcision.html

OBEDIENCE IS THE REVOLUTION

Yahusha was among His own, living in a culture far different than what spread around the Earth after Constantine's council at Nicaea in 325. The adversary (ha shatan) has deceived the whole world (Rev. 12:9-10). If I were a servant of ha shatan, how would it work out for my boss if I teach people to be restored to Yahuah by teaching them the **real Name**, call on it for the forgiveness of their sins, and **to obey His Commandments**? Would it not be more logical for them to never learn the real Name, and be told to ignore the Commandments? Yahusha was upset with the teaching authority because they taught men's traditions in place of Yahuah's Commandments. People are trained to disobey Yahuah instead. Have You been immersed by someone in the fake name Jesus, or have you called on the only Name under heaven given among men by which we must be delivered, Yahusha? (Acts 4:12)

Only Yahusha has the power to immerse a person, men have no power to deliver, redeem, or change a human heart from being disobedient. If we are His sheep, He will drive us to the still waters because we hear His voice, and will not follow other shepherds anywhere. Our old inclination to sin is left behind in the waters of immersion, and His Spirit gives us life, sealing us in His Name.
https://youtu.be/aCzTnW7RQBA

Are you ready to become an ambassador of the coming reign of Yahusha? The core misunderstanding in Christian teachings concerns the old way (animal blood), and the new way (Yahusha's blood). The answer is found at **Dt. 31:26**, and relates with the text at **Hebrews 8:13**. The Truth will set you free.

IMMERSION: Yahusha seals us for the day of redemption

Between your birth and your death, what is the most important thing you can do? Apologize to Yahuah, ask His forgiveness; be immersed. This video on Lew White's channel asks:
Were You Baptized Into A Circus? https://youtu.be/lr7eh_Yh4wo

RAPTURE?
The video essay linked below explains the origins of the rapture ideas, who originated them, and how they became popularized. The Latin word *raptus* gives us the word rapere, rapier, and rape. Here's the link to the youtube video: **https://youtu.be/lp8AA-Fjk8w**

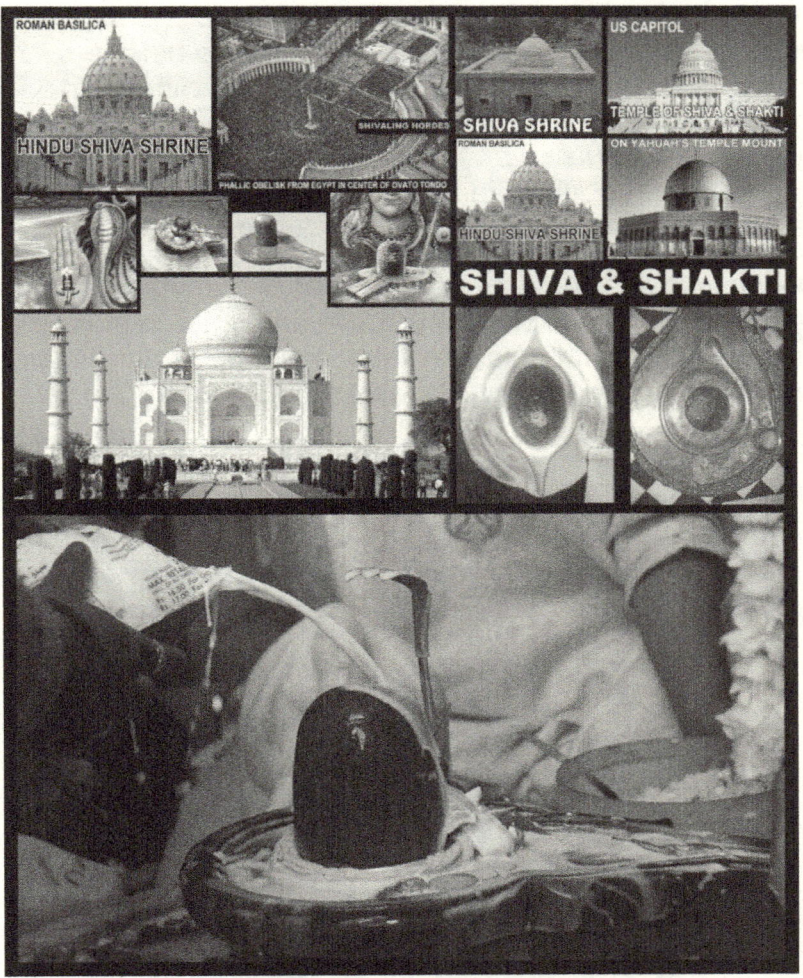

What happened on the **Silk Road** did not stay on the Silk Road; It has spilled-over everywhere - don't get any on you!

The Information Age is enabling many to learn about the arrival of Shiva worship via the Silk Road out of India around 200 BCE. The crescent and star, circumambulating around the object of worship, a shivalingam (black stone), domes, pillars, prayer beads (tears of Shiva, and repetitive prayers), and other blended customs reveal a great deal of syncretism has occurred, being adopted from Hindu traditions. Most capital buildings around the Earth are modeled after the architecture of Shiva shrines. Compare the Taj Mahal, St. Peter's Cathedral, and U.S. Capital buildings side-by-side.
Mahadeva (Hindi, meaning *great god*) is a ***title*** for Shiva, and seems very familiar in meaning to the Islamic takbir, *god is greatest*.
The One true Alahim indeed is the only Alahim to believers.
To love one another, especially those who differ with us, is a worthy goal to pursue. In 2015, a Muslim cleric in India named Qasmi claimed that **Lord Shiva** was the first prophet of Islam. From all appearances, the traditions in Islam and Hinduism are cut from the same cloth. **www.fossilizedcustoms.com/allah.html**

I've spoken with missionaries sent by their denominations into remote places who all explain how they cannot reach those who support their work, but those they teach love the Truth. If their supporters learned what they are teaching they would lose their jobs.
Denominational lines and men's doctrines have blinded hundreds of millions of people. Roman excavations beneath Catholic basilicas reveal they are built on top of underground **Mithras temples**. Welcome to the **mysterious world of syncretism**; *everything is blended together.* **www.fossilizedcustoms.com/syncretism.html**

Circular Firing Squad

Gangrene is rotting the body of Yahusha (2Tim. 2:14-19).

Yahusha's sheep follow and listen only to their Shepherd, and He is calling others to join Him all the time.

No one is worthy, and yet He is crying out at the doorposts and gates constantly. He is the only One able to write them on our hearts, circumcising us with a love for obedience.

Through my own persecution I've learned what damage can be done by spreading information about others who are alive on the planet, since if they have not yet joined to Yahuah, they may yet do so.

Through bad teachings, the Natsarim are becoming more like a *circular firing squad* every day.

We all must be breaking Yahusha's heart, but as He separates His sheep from His goats, it remains His decision, not the decision of the sheep or the goats. Before we judge others, or decide to pass along gossip on anyone, or read the reports, consider these scriptures before you do:

Yaqub (James) 1:26, 4:11 ... 2Kor 12:20 ... Prov. 10:18

"May the words of my mouth and the meditation in my heart be pleasing in your sight Yahuah, my Rock and my Redeemer." Psalm 19:14

Remember: love one another.

This is how the world will know we are followers of Yahusha.

We are not to behave as a circular firing squad, but build-up one another in love. This rejection of one another must stop.

CIRCULAR FIRING SQUAD
Natsarim Search Team

Foreigners who join to Yahuah are to be treated the same, without pointing out any distinctions.

Skin is a distinction. We are not to point it out, no matter who we think is the right skin color.
Ruth is in the line of Yahuah's human body, and she was a Moabite, of the BEL (Baal) worshipping Molok variety.
She engrafted. Our Alahim became her Alahim, and His people became her people. There's no questioning it, it's done.

Vatican Forbids The Name Yahuah
A Vatican Bull announced 8-26-2008 by the Congregation for Divine Worship and the Sacraments (updated name for the Inquisition) prohibits anyone uttering the Name Yahuah, but that's too bad. We'll read their bull below. Yahusha's Natsarim have always ignored Nicolaitanes, and so Yahuah's Name is being shouted from the rooftops. Maybe the Grand Inquisitor will convert and call on the Name above all names. Yahusha said, **"You will not see Me again until you say, 'BARUK HABA BASHEM YAHUAH!'"**
(Mt. 23:39, Luke 13;35) www.fossilizedcustoms.com/beast.html

HERE'S THE BULL
A papal bull issued a special directive to all bishops 8-26-2008, and this is the full text of it under this heading from catholic.org:

Vatican Says No 'Yahweh' In Songs, Prayers At Catholic Masses
"The Vatican has reiterated a directive that the name of God revealed in the tetragrammaton YHWH is not to be pronounced in Catholic liturgy or in music. Catholics at worship should neither sing nor pronounce the name of God as Yahweh, the Vatican has said, citing the authority of Jewish and Christian practice. The instruction came in a June 29 letter to Catholic bishops' conferences around the world from the Vatican's top liturgical body, the **Congregation for Divine Worship and the Sacraments, by an explicit directive of Pope Benedict XVI.**

'In recent years, the practice has crept in of pronouncing the God of Israel's proper name,' the letter noted, referring to the four-consonant Hebrew Tetragrammaton, YHWH. (double – U is a new letter)
That name is commonly pronounced as Yahweh, though other versions include Jaweh and Yehovah.
But such pronunciation violates long-standing Jewish tradition, the Vatican reminded bishops.
'As an expression of the infinite greatness and majesty of God, (the name) was held to be unpronounceable and hence was replaced

during the reading of sacred Scripture by means of the use of an alternate name: Adonai, which means Lord," the Congregation said. That practice continued with Christianity, the letter explained, recalling the 'church's tradition, from the beginning, that the sacred Tetragrammaton was never pronounced in the Christian context nor translated into any of the languages into which the Bible was translated.'

Invoking a Vatican document from 2001, the Congregation reminded bishops that the name Yahweh in Catholic worship should be replaced by the Latin Dominus (Lord) or a word 'equivalent in meaning' in the local language.

The Vatican's move will require changes in a number of hymns and prayers currently used in American churches, but not to the Mass itself, said the U.S. bishops' top liturgical official." [end quote]

The *Congregation for Divine Worship and the Sacraments* is the updated name for the *Inquisition*. This bull is a directive to not utter the Name Yahuah. This quote states the four-lettered Name in Hebrew consists of four *consonants*, but Yusef Ben MatithYahu (Flavius Josephus) said they were four *vowels*. What's a vowel?

VOWEL: A vowel is a letter sounded without using the lips, teeth, upper teeth on lower lip, or tongue on the roof of the mouth; only the breath and mouth cavity are used.

CONSONANT: A consonant is a letter making use of the lips, teeth, upper teeth on lower lip, or tongue on the roof of the mouth. Psalms 118:26 is quoted by Yahusha at Mt. 23:39 when He said, "You will not see Me again until you say, 'BARUK HABA BASHEM YAHUAH."

Does Yahuah really not want anyone to call on His Name? This is not a hard answer to find. For example, this text is very clear:

"Pour out Your wrath on the Guyim Who have not known You, And on reigns that have not called on Your Name." (Psalms 79:6)

Are There Consonants In Our Creator's Name?

The whole world is in the control of the evil one, but that control is slipping. Yahusha is awakening us to the misdirection of those who teach us. They are so disconnected from the will of Yahusha they actually pretend to believe He is offended when we obey His Turah.

Even those who claim to teach His Name have infiltrated our thoughts with misdirection. Reasoning together with Yahuah, we can see there is no way we can reconcile what the Word says with what the teaching authorities are saying to everyone.
Only days before being killed, Yahusha was riding on a donkey as He entered an excited, vivacious crowd screaming,

"BARUK HABA BASHEM YAHUAH!"

The teaching authority was aghast, and still is.
We will not see Him again until we say,
"BARUK HABA BASHEM YAHUAH!" It is impossible to obey men who forbid using His Name, and expect to see Him again. In the Vatican's bull forbidding the utterance of the Name, the four-lettered Name is mistakenly described as *four consonants*, but this is not true, they are *vowels*.
If you take time to reason how the true Name consists of four vowels, you will conclude that the letter V is never a vowel, it is a consonant. Yusef Ben MatithYahu *(Flavius Josephus)* said the Name was written with **four vowels**.
We are being guided by the Spirit of Truth Himself, or we are being misdirected by another spirit. Be careful how you hear, and reason together with Yahuah.
Our approval is not from men, nor should we seek men's approval. There are no niqqud marks or *phonemes* found on any of the Dead Sea Scrolls. We must prove all things, and hold fast to what is good. (1Thess. 5:21)
An irreconcilable phonetic spelling, YEHO**V**AH, uses one consonant, and has Masoretic influences as well.
Remember Malaki 3:16-18; Yahuah is listening to us as we speak to one another about His Name!

www.fossilizedcustoms.com/name.html

Our Teachers Have Withheld the Key Of Knowledge
We were told, but now in the last days we understand. We will not see Him again until we say one simple sentence (Mt. 23:39).
If you go to a teacher or pastor and ask if there is such a thing as a *"sin of omission,"* and he says **yes**, follow-up with another question. Ask if he knows what the Name of our Creator is, and if he has omitted revealing it. How will they call on the Name *unless they are sent someone to tell them what it is?* If you have read and

understood this, then it is your obligation to warn them - they are sleeping soundly, and the Natsarim are shouting from the rooftops.
Baruk haba bashem Yahuah
(blessed is the one coming in the Name of Yahuah).
www.fossilizedcustoms.com/third.html

Are We Giving Yahuah Our Very Best? (Yahusha inspired Ray Todd)
Dt. 17:14-20 instructs all kings to write the Turah of Alahim. And, as priests under Yahusha, our Melkitsedek High priest, we should know and teach the **Name** of Yahuah and His **Turah**.
Yahusha wrote a love for His Turah on my heart. Yahusha put the desire on my heart to translate the BYNV, which restores the Name, and to teach the phonology of the letters more accurately. Most prefaces openly admit the translators replaced the Name with the device "LORD" - a pattern *adopted from tradition*. Rather than pronounce the Name, the Yahudim would say **Aduni** (lord); the Greek in turn translated this as **Kurios** (lord); the Latin Vulgate in turn used **Dominus** (lord); and the Anglican Catholic KJV used the Latin-to-English to teach the whole world our Creator's Name is **LORD**. AliYahu met the Bel-worshippers at Karmel to settle that issue long ago. 1 Kings 18 shows us who is Alahim, and LORD, Dominus, Kurios, Aduni, or Bel doesn't work for Yahuah.
Bel literally means *lord* (concordance **#1167**).
As a brother once described it, we seem to only give Yahuah our second-best, *or worse*. He wants us to give Him our very best.

Yahuah Or Bel? . . . Yahusha Or Jesus?
The question is exactly the same today as it was in the time of AliYahu at Mt. Karmel (1Kings 18). What is His Name, if you know? Signs and wonders are for the benefit of unbelievers, of course, but if any miracle ever happens, it is only Yahusha in the person doing His wonders through them. His Name is not a magical spell, but His presence can do anything. Unbelievers tried to use His Name to cast out demons, but then they quickly learned they were not sealed, and the outcome for them was not good.
Acts 16:13-16 explains it: **"But certain roving Yahudi exorcists took it upon themselves to call the Name of Aduni Yahusha over those who had wicked ruachs, saying, 'We exorcise you by Yahusha whom Paul proclaims.' And there were seven sons of a certain Skua, a Yahudi chief priest, who were doing this.**

And the wicked ruach answering, said, 'Yahusha I know, and Paul I know, but who are you?' And the man in whom the wicked ruach was leaped on them, overpowered them, and prevailed against them, so that they fled out of that house naked and wounded."

The most amazing miracle of all is Yahusha's Truth being received into the heart of a person, and changing them forever. He gives them His eyesight when they go to water to be immersed, and call on His Name. This seals them for the day of our redemption, when the dead in Yahusha rise first, and we who are alive are changed, clothed with immortality. If you will take the first step in returning to His Covenant, He will run to you to welcome you, prodigal child! *The Father of the house has been watching the path for your return every moment of every day.* All you must do is know He's there waiting for you, and start coming home to Him.

HE-SUS means *the horse* in the ears of those who speak Eberith (Hebrew). Was Yahusha called *JESUS* to His face by anyone? Or *IESOUS?* What would these words mean to any one of His followers? The Truth is, these words were invented much later by an interloper. The true Eberith script is available to view inside the Hekal Sefer (Shrine of the Book) in Yerushalom under glass, and photos of the Name are easy to find all over the Internet. The Greek is a translation. When Paul spoke Greek to the commander arresting him at Acts 21:37, the man said, *"Can you speak Greek?"* Eberith is mentioned 11 times in the book of Acts, Aramith is never mentioned. The Truth is pouring out everywhere into the world suddenly, and false teachers are scrambling to hold their positions as people's eyes are opening to the steeples, domes, indoor altars, miters, stoles, collars, sacraments, haloes, processions, forbidding calling on the Name, Sun-day, statues, and all the idolatry behind the fertility celebrations keeping the economy of the whole world turning over. The last Natsarim are crying out to wake up those who will listen, because when Yahusha comes out of His place, all the world will be in anguish. The disguises people hide behind to trick people are already growing thread-bare. Look again at why the Earth (arets) will be utterly laid-waist when Yahusha returns:

"See, Yahuah is making the arets empty and making it waste, and shall overturn its surface, and shall scatter abroad its inhabitants. And it shall be – as with the people so with the

priest, as with the servant so with his Aduni, as with the female servant so with her mistress, as with the buyer so with the seller, as with the lender so with the borrower, as with the creditor so with the debtor; the arets is completely emptied and utterly plundered, for Yahuah has spoken this word.
The arets shall mourn and wither, the world shall languish and wither, the haughty people of the arets shall languish.
For the arets has been defiled under its inhabitants, because they have transgressed the Turoth, changed the law, broken the everlasting covenant. Therefore a curse shall consume the arets, and those who dwell in it be punished. Therefore the inhabitants of the arets shall be burned, and few men shall be left." – YashaYahu (Isaiah) 24:1-6

We Have To Dig & Hunt

Can we call our Maker whatever name we choose, as if we have the authority to do such a thing?
Psalm 102:18 says His Name is written so a generation yet to be created might be able to call on the Name Yah.
If Yahusha performs a miracle in a fake Name, it is because He **winks at our ignorance**. Paul realized how ignorant, yet pious, the philosophers were in the situation at Acts 17. We would not want to call any miracle *demonic*, but we should study further to examine the truth of the Name before we deny it. The miracle is far less important than His Name, and we should never put Yahusha to the test on such a basis. He wants us to study to show ourselves approved by Him, not make ourselves look important in the eyes of others without any effort. His Name is precious, and not a circus act. Definitely, the Spirit of Yahusha can do as He pleases, even if we don't know His Name. Ask Him to reveal His one and only Name to you, but don't ask Him for a sign. Read Acts 4:12, and put that together with YashaYahu (Isaiah) 42:8, Psalm 102:18, and Proverbs 30:4, and you will be able to purge all the leaven of what men have put in your mind, if you will believe what you are reading. Don't trust any transliteration of the Name until you test everything thoroughly. Look at the Hebrew script, and you will see His Name.

TRANSLITERATIONS

	6,823 YAHUAH	216 YAHUSHA	2 YAHUSHUA	1 Y'SHUA
HEBREW	ᴎYᴎZ	OWYᴎZ	OYWYᴎZ	OYWZ
ARAMAIC	יהוה	יהושע	יהושוע	ישוע
GREEK	IAOUE	IHSOUS		
LATIN	IEHOUAH	IESU		

AT HEBREWS 4 AND ACTS 7 THE SAME GREEK LETTERING IS USED FOR "JOSHUA" AND "JESUS" - IHSOUS
THIS IS CONFIRMATION BOTH WERE CALLED YAHUSHA IN HEBREW
TORAH INSTITUTE

Yahuah Is Restoring Maiden Yisharal

The **old** (obsolete) **covenant** was written on a **scroll** (sefer) and placed **beside** the ark (Dt. 31:26), and was the priesthood's instructions for offering animal blood. It is further described at Hebrews 8:13. Yahusha's blood is the perfect offering completing the requirement for atonement, and is the end (shalom, fulfillment, finish, completion) of the old covenant. The old covenant was the **schoolmaster** which pointed to Yahusha's offering. The eternal Covenant of love defines sin, and was originally written in stone tablets by the finger of Yahuah. It is our marriage ketubah for His maiden bride (ashah, wife). We are His first-fruits, obeying the Commandments of Yahuah and holding to the testimony of Yahusha (branches of His teachings): **Natsarim**.

Whom Do You Seek?

If you are trying to be restored to favor with Yahusha, why are you sitting in a pew under a steeple listening to lies?

Do you not know? Have you not heard?
The Scriptures begin and end with a marriage; everything written in between is a record of Yahuah looking for the ashah (wife, woman) He created for Himself. Teachers have caused great confusion, but He is breaking their *spiel* (spell) that clouded our thinking, and a remnant has chosen to obey Him.

**TURNING ASIDE TO MYTHS HAPPENS
WHAT COULD POSSIBLY GO WRONG?
CAUSE: 2 TIM 4   EFFECT: MAL 4   FOSSILIZEDCUSTOMS.COM**

While His eyes roam to and fro across the Earth for His woman's obedience, she is not so concerned with looking for Him, but rather she is looking for more scrolls, and more scrolls.
*People want **evidence**, Yahuah wants **obedience**.*
Qoheleth 12:13-14 says there is no end of the writing of books, but the end of the matter is to obey Yahuah's Commandments; this is the objective of all mankind.
He told us they were not difficult, nor are they far off; they are very near (Dt. 30:13).
Yahuah has not spoken in secret. (YashaYahu / Isaiah 45:19)
Rather than focusing on stumbling across a forgotten secret yet to be discovered, or a map to a huge treasure hidden underground, we should be most interested in testing ourselves to see if we are walking as Yahusha walked. If we know Him, we have already been sealed for the day of our redemption, and have overcome the world. The true Natsarim are breathing out the literal words of Yahusha, Who lives in them, and are recognized by those words. If they disobey, or tell others to disobey, do not listen to them, or their many footnotes that argue against the text.

We Are His Witnesses, That He Is Alahim
YashaYahu (Isaiah) **43:1-13** (This name means: *Deliverer is Yahuah*)
"But now, thus said Yahuah, your Creator, O Yaqub, and He who formed you, O Yisharal, 'Do not fear, for I have redeemed you. I have called you by your name, you are Mine. When you pass through the mayim, I am with you; and through rivers, they do not overflow you. When you walk through fire, you are not scorched, and a flame does not burn you. For I am Yahuah your Alahim, the qodesh One of Yisharal, your Deliverer; I gave Mitsrim for your ransom, Kush and Seba in your place. Since you were precious in

My eyes, you have been esteemed, and I have loved you. And I give men in your place, and peoples for your life. **Do not fear, for I am with you.** I shall bring your seed from the east, and gather you from the west. I shall say to the north, "Give them up!" And to the south, "Do not keep them back!" Bring My sons from afar, and My daughters from the ends of the arets – all those who are called by My Name, whom I have created, formed, even made for My esteem. He shall bring out a blind people who have eyes, and deaf ones who have ears. All the guyim shall be assembled, and the peoples be gathered. Who among them says this, and show us former events? Let them give their witnesses, to be declared right; or let them hear and say, "It is truth."
'You are My witnesses,' says Yahuah, 'And My servant whom I have chosen, so that you know and believe Me, and understand that **I am He**. Before Me there was no Al formed, nor after Me there is none. **I, I am Yahuah, and besides Me there is no deliverer.** I, I have declared and delivered, and made known, and there was no foreign mighty one among you. And you are My witnesses,' says Yahuah, 'that **I am Al**. Even from the yom **I am He**, and no one delivers out of My hand.'" – YashaYahu (Isaiah) 43:1-13

Why Do We Have The Scriptures?
Psalm 102:18 tells us, **"This was written for a generation to come, so that a people to be created praise Yah."**
Yahuah wrote His Name in His Writings of Truth far more than any other single word, and it consists of *four vowels*.
Teachers are insisting there are no written vowels in the Hebrew texts, so the Masoretes had to invent vowel marks in the 8th century. The evidence is overwhelming that we are being lied to.
When teachers call the script of Babel (which are Aramith, not Eberith letters) "*Hebrew*," they are often the same people explaining how there are rules to follow in order to correctly pronounce the Hebrew language. A script is the method used to write in, and a *language* may be written in many different kinds of *scripts*.
If we write in a script few people can read, then we can make the majority believe whatever we tell them it says. The Internet is filled with all kinds of teachings, and people to teach them. Most of them are passing on traditions they learned, and the errors have become repeated so often, they are embraced as the Truth. Some know the

Truth, but keep making excuses. What we have here is a classic example of misdirection, and **equivocation**.
Casuistry
(*casuistry* - the use of clever but unsound reasoning) is often used by teachers who claim the four lettered Name is made up of **consonants**. They use special cases to think about stuff.
"The first to present his case seems right, until another another comes and questions him." (Proverbs 18:17)

NEWS FLASH!
ALEF IS AN "A"

HUH?

𝓎 △ 𝟰 ADAM
ADAM MEANS RED GROUND

𝆑 4 𝟰 ARETS
ARETS IS HEBREW FOR EARTH, SOIL, OR LAND

𝓎 ⊐ ϶ (𝟰 ALAHIM
ALAHIM MEANS ELEVATED, HIGH, UPWARD, MIGHTY ONE

AND IT'S A VOWEL

𝓎 ϶ 𝟰 𝟫 𝟰 ABRAHIM
ABRAHIM MEANS FATHER OF NATIONS, MULTITUDES

They will defend their position (their *case*) by declaring that those who promote a wide array of different pronunciations than they use *don't know anything about Hebrew*.
The fact is, the Name of Yahuah is **four vowels**.
It's obvious they are vowels, because they have no hard-attack or glottal-stop when the letters are pronounced in the Name.
If the lips, teeth, tongue on the roof of the mouth, or upper teeth on lower lip is involved, it is a consonant. If you hear "YEHO<u>V</u>AH," the **V** is a **consonant**, therefore it is an incorrect pronunciation.
The *YEHO* is a separate problem, and also incorrect.
Since we don't have any recordings of how Hebrew words sounded, we can review the written record of someone that lived while the Temple (Hekel) was standing, and definitely DID know how to utter the Hebrew language. His name is Yusef Ben MatithYahu, but the scholarly world has been teaching us his name is "Flavius Josephus." This word should be uttered YUSEF, not Josephus.

Yusef Ben MatithYahu (Flavius Josephus) in his War of the Yahudim book 5, chapter 5 v.7 states:
"A mitre also of fine linen encompassed his head, which was tied by a blue ribbon, about which there was another golden crown, in which was engraven the sacred name - it consists of four vowels."

(see **Glossary** for definitions of a consonant and a vowel).

The narrator in one Hebrew teaching presentation goes on a "rules" explanation of consonants and vowels, and seems to not be aware of the fact the Name has no consonants. "Closed syllables" (CvC) and "open syllables" (Cv) is used as the vehicle to explain the pronunciation of the Name, *and yet no pronunciation is ever offered.* Instead, a *substituted translation* is emphasized, teaching how the word name generically refers to an *abstract trait* or *characteristic,* and not a concrete method of identification.

Our word **noun** is defined as *the name of something* in a sentence. It is not the *characteristic* of something, it identifies a **specific thing** by *naming it.*

The word **character** in Latin is **persona**, and means **MASK**.
I'm not trying to use cleverness to deceive, I'm telling it straight.
If we do not **call** (QARA) **on the Name of our Creator,** but instead **mask His Name** for the sake of unity, we cannot truly know the **identity** of the one we are calling on. This presentation leads nowhere, except to show contempt for those who pursue the pronunciation of the Name, which Natsarim are guardians of.
He accuses us of spreading chaos.

When Yahuah states the following, He is not referring to His *character,* but *His real and only Name:*

YashaYahu (Is.) 42:8: **"I am Yahuah, that is My Name, and My esteem I do not give to another, nor My praise to idols."**

Exodus 9:16: **"And for this reason I have raised you up, in order to show you My power, and in order to declare My Name in all the earth."**

The Farah (pharaoh) did not know Yahuah:

Exodus 5:2: **"And Pharaoh said, 'Who is Yahuah, that I should obey His voice to let Yisharal go? I do not know Yahuah, nor am I going to let Yisharal go.'"**

What if AliYahu (commonly known as Elijah) had called upon some **substituted Name** at Mount Karmel?

Some teachers also promote the letter shapes sometimes called proto-Sinaitic script of the Hyksos, a primitive adaptation of Egyptian hieroglyphics. This script was never developed beyond a handful of letters based on hieroglyphs, the bulk of which discovered on cave walls believed to be turquoise mines in the Sinai peninsula.

They were working in turquoise mines near the ancient ruins of an Egyptian temple dedicated to the goddess Hathor, the mistress of turquoise. You can research this script and the site called **Serabit ha'Khadem**.

No one has ever discovered **Yod-Hay-Uau-Hay** written in such letters, yet many Natsarim are promoting it all over the place on hats, shirts, and web designs. The Hyksos were Kananites, and imitated what they saw on Egyptian temple writings. This is all there is to the origin of such letter shapes. Yahuah didn't write in the script of the Egyptians, or the Hyksos, this is a hoax being taught. No matter who says it, or how often you may hear it, these are not the original forms for the Hebrew letters, or their precursers.

They are Egyptian in origin, and crudely copied by Kananites, a people known as the **Hyksos** working at Serabit ha'Khadem, the site of the temple of Hathor, the Egyptian mistress of turquoise:

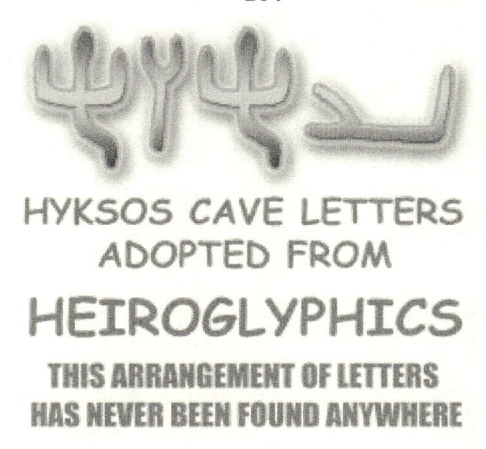

HYKSOS CAVE LETTERS
ADOPTED FROM

HEIROGLYPHICS

**THIS ARRANGEMENT OF LETTERS
HAS NEVER BEEN FOUND ANYWHERE**

ᴲ Y ᴲ ℤ

WINDOW HOOK   WINDOW   HAND

The black letters above show the real palaeo-Hebrew script, mistakenly referred to by the Greek term *Phoenician* by modern scholars. The first to use the term *Phoenician* was the 5th-century BCE historian known as **Herodotus**. A Greek himself, he made up a word based on his own Greek language to describe the **sea people** that lived in the land occupied by Yisharal, the Tyrians, and Sidonians. Herodotus described their territory by the term *Phoenicia* which means **date palm** in Greek, from two words **Phoen-nike**. The Romans turned the word into **Punic**, fighting the colonies of Yisharal in their Punic wars.

The authentic Eberith script used by the ancient Hebrews is shown on the next page:

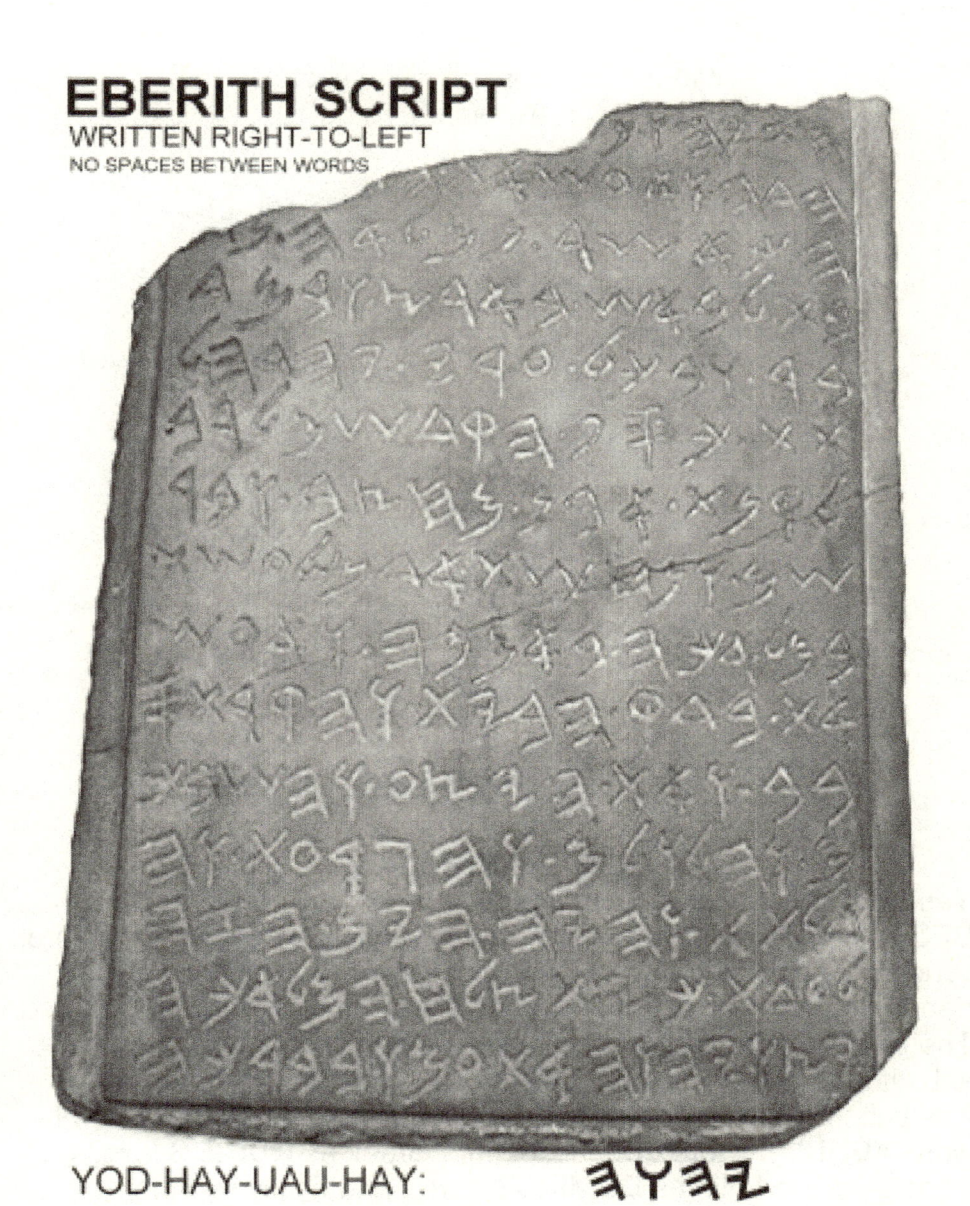

EBERITH SCRIPT
WRITTEN RIGHT-TO-LEFT
NO SPACES BETWEEN WORDS

YOD-HAY-UAU-HAY: ᴣYᴣZ

The Name is on the bottom line in the photo above. People are mixing things together and making Yahuah's Name into sentences formed around what the letters seem to mean to them. Some look up the definitions of the names of prophets to form a story-line, using their imaginations exactly as a medium would use her Tarot cards. We were told not to do this, nor are we to listen to those who use the Sun, Moon, and stars to teach us secrets.

Yahuah has not spoken in secret.
Read Dt. 4, especially verse 19.

IS BAAL NIMROD?
Yes, and all Sun deities are babbled forms of this rebel's name. BEL (beth-ayin-lamed) can be a proper noun (name), and it means lord. When not used as a proper noun it can mean *husband* or *owner* depending on the context when used in Scripture.

The English word lord is not usually a proper noun, but if used to substitute the Name of Yahuah, LORD becomes a proper noun. The substitutions used for Yahuah's Name began with the Eberith word **ADUNI** (my lord), translated into Greek as **KURIOS** (lord), translated into Latin as **DOMINUS** (lord), and finally into the Anglican Catholic KJV as **LORD**. Names are not to be *translated*, but *transliterated*. They removed Yahuah's Name, and this is what He says about that:

"I have heard what the prophets have said who prophesy falsehood in My Name, saying, 'I have dreamed, I have dreamed!' Till when shall it be in the heart of the prophets? – the prophets of falsehood and prophets of the deceit of their

own heart, who try to make My people forget My Name by their dreams which everyone relates to his neighbor, as their fathers forgot My Name for Bel." YirmeYahu / Jer. 23:25-27 BYNV
www.fossilizedcustoms.com/nimrod.html

Blessed is He Who comes in the Name of Yahuah, not BEL. Scripture *begins* and *ends* with a marriage, and is a love record of Yahuah creating for Himself a new thing, called mankind. Because He knows the end from the beginning, His first-fruits share this undertaking with Him, to increase knowledge and fruitful obedience. When the **reign of Babel** falls in one day (the elements will burn), and we Natsarim will hear Yahuah **singing over us.**
In the following pages watch the Word reveal the end of the towers / steeples, the burning of the entire arets, and the emergence of Yahuah's bride from the pages of prophecy. This is how Yahuah awakens His bride and gathers us from the nations, turning-back our captivity:
TsefanYah (Zephaniah) 3:3-20:
'"Woe to her who is rebellious and defiled, the oppressing city! She did not heed the voice, she did not accept instruction, she did not trust in Yahuah, she did not draw near to her Alahim. Her rulers in her midst are roaring lions, her judges are evening wolves, they shall leave no bone until morning. Her prophets are reckless, treacherous men. Her priests have profaned the qodesh place, they have done violence to the Turah. Yahuah is obedient in her midst, He does no disobedience. Morning by morning He brings His lawfulness to light, it has not been lacking, yet the unobedient one knows no shame. I have cut off guyim (nations), their corner towers are in ruins. I have made their streets deserted, with no one passing by. Their cities are destroyed, without man, without inhabitant. I have said, "Only fear Me, accept instruction." And her dwelling would not be cut off, all that I have appointed for her. But they rose up early, they corrupted all their actions. 'Therefore wait for Me,' says Yahuah, 'until the yom I rise up for plunder. For My decision is to gather guyim, to assemble reigns, to pour out on them My rage, all my burning wrath. *For by the fire of My jealousy all the arets shall be consumed. For then I shall turn to the peoples a clean lip, so that they all call on the Name of Yahuah, to serve Him with one shoulder.* From beyond the rivers

of Kush my worshippers, the daughter of My dispersed ones, shall bring My offering. In that yom you shall not be put to shame for any of your actions in which you have transgressed against Me, for then I shall remove from your midst your proud exulting ones, and you shall no more be haughty in My qodesh mountain. But I shall leave in your midst an oppressed and poor people, and they shall trust in the Name of Yahuah. The remnant of Yisharal shall do no disobedience and speak no falsehood, nor is a tongue of deceit found in their mouth. For they shall feed their flocks and lie down, with none to frighten them.

Shout for joy, daughter of Tsiun! Shout, Yisharal! Be glad and rejoice with all your heart, daughter of Yerushalim! Yahuah has turned aside your judgments. He has faced your enemy.

The King of Yisharal, Yahuah, is in your midst.
No longer need you fear evil. In that yom it shall be said to Yerushalim, **"Do not fear, Tsiun, do not let your hands be weak. Yahuah your Alahim in your midst, is mighty to save. He rejoices over you with joy, He is silent in His love, He rejoices over you with singing."**

I shall gather those who grieve about the appointed place, who are among you, to whom its reproach is a burden. See, I am dealing with all those afflicting you at that time. And I shall save the lame, and gather those who were cast out. And I shall give them for a praise and for a name in all the arets where they were put to shame. *At that time I shall bring you in, even at the time I gather you, for I shall give you for a name, and for a praise, among all the peoples of the arets, when I turn back your captivity before your eyes,'* said Yahuah."

The Spirit of Error

If one of the first Natsarim were to somehow be taken from their time and place and brought forward to see what people think and do now, they would not recognize, or believe what they would see.

If a Seminary professor from any Christian institution were to stand next to one of first Natsarim and compare notes, one could honestly say their walk <u>is</u> found in the Scripture of Truth, but the other would find no evidence of their walk in Scripture. The Christian would be unable to do anything the other practiced due to men's traditions completely overwhelming their world view. Obeying Commandments is legalistic to the Christian walk, yet the Natsarim establish the idea.

How are Natsarim different from Christians?
Both claim to follow the same Person, yet in practice differ in every way.
It is impossible to repent while continuing to sin.
We are ambassadors sent to free the prisoners imprisoned by the stronghold of faulty thinking. Christian doctrines promote sin. They have received a spirit of error.
To be legal is heretical in their minds, and accomplishes the will of Nimrod, Izebel, Antiochus Epiphanes, and Constantine.
In Scripture, there is no such thing as a way of living called CHRISTIANITY, but it's practices can be found. All the heathens we read about in Scripture were doing the things Christians are doing today. People need to see things from Yahuah's perspective, not men's traditional view. Those who worship Yahuah do so in Truth, not through religion. Truth is reality, tradition is religion.

WHO OR WHAT ARE CHRISTIANS?
Without knowing it, Christians are followers of a Greco-Roman culture of names, terms, and festivals, all adopted intact from pagan sources, yet adapted and mixed carefully with ideas and people from the Hebrew Scriptures.
Mixing together the practices and beliefs of an indigenous population is missionary adaptation, called **syncretism**. These heresies from the *reign of Babel* began to take root through the teachings of Simon Magus, and through councils eventually became the basis for the teaching authority known as the Catechetical School at Alexandria (C.S.A.) under its first headmaster, Pantaenus in 190 CE.
This institution set up the frameword that eventually came to dominate the beliefs and practices of the entire western world.
The ***Great Schism*** of 1054 CE produced the rift between the western empire Roman Catholic Magisterium at Rome and Eastern Orthodox Catholicism. Later the Reformation in the 16th century further fragmented the movement when the nobility rejected the papal authority at Rome; but much error remained from the adherence to the early church fathers and their writings. These church fathers persecuted and despised the first followers of Yahusha, the

Natsarim, and wrote about us. They considered us heretics because we obey the Torah.

Every detail of **Scriptural observance** was omitted by the church fathers, and replaced with new observances.

With skillfully-crafted reasoning over many centuries, the formerly pagan observances were camouflaged or wrapped in new meanings, believing to be cleansed of their filth, and now loved and cherished by their LORD. Yahusha would never teach the things they do.

Examples:

Sacraments - Yahuah never commanded them, hinted at them indirectly, or mentioned any such thing. They add to the Torah, against Dt. 12.

Sun-day - the Day of the Sun. Many other even stranger festivals were invented, all being adaptations from former Sun worship.

SUNDAY ORIGINS
SUN WORSHIP'S SPECIAL DAY
Lew White

The cult of Sun worshippers at Alexandria, Egypt worshipped Osiris and called themselves Christians in the 2nd century BCE by bowing to cross-shapes, used by Sun worshipping pagans world-wide.

Most all the headmasters at Alexandria were former worshippers of the Sun. They adopted all their former practices and re-packaged them to be easily consumed by unregenerate pagans.

Easter was one of them, and they didn't even change the name!

TORAH INSTITUTE
WHO IS EASTER?

SHE IS GAIA, ASTAROTH, ISHTAR ARTEMIS, VENUS, APHRODITE SEMIRAMIS, NATURE, GREAT MOTHER FRIGGA, LIBERTAS, EOSTRE, DURGA HATHOR, QUEEN OF HEAVEN

Easter Day - the Pagan festival of the impregnation of Mother Earth by the rays of the springtime sun. Ishtar, Ostara, Astarte, Eostre, Asherah, Eastron, Ashtaroth, and other names were used for this Pagan deity. It became adopted to refer to Yahusha's day of resurrection.

Easter is the proper name of the Pagan Queen of heaven.
(Google the words: Ashtaroth, Easter)

Christmas - The winter solstice festival, commemorated as the nativity of the sun, re-thought by Dionysius Exiguus in 525 CE, now promoted as the birthday of the Mashiak. Wreaths (wombs), trees (phalluses), tinsel (semen) & balls (testes) were used to observe the sexual aspects of this pagan ritual.

The tree was an altar where offerings were placed for the deity (Asherah). Those not studying won't care about any of this, and your family will think you're crazy.

The womb wreaths and trees represented Asherah and Bel. This is a practice inherited from the ancient Canaanites, specifically Izabel (Jezebel). The bel in Iza<u>bel</u> is that deity, and bel in Hebrew means LORD. *There's an accident up ahead; are the red flags waving yet?*

Ultimate determination: Come out of her - and be gentle and kind as you help them.
Mashiak Yahusha observed **none** of these practices; **pagans did**.
1 Yahukanon / John 2:3-6 (Yahukanon means: *Yahuah is kind*)
"We know that we have come to know Him if we obey His Commands. The man who says, 'I know him,' but does not do what He commands is a liar, and the Truth is not in him. But if anyone obeys His Word, Alahim's love is truly made complete in him. This is how we know we are in Him: <u>Whoever claims to live in Him must walk as Yahusha did</u>."

Natsarim walk as Yahusha did, we do the things He did, and observe the observances He observed, according to the Word of Yahuah. He lived as our example. So, how does it become appropriate for us to ignore all the things He did, and embrace Christmas, Easter, and Sun-day, observances borrowed from pagan cultures?
Will He find the belief on the Earth when He returns?
This brief comparison is intended to expose the darkness and deception that has overtaken the world.

"For you were once darkness, but now you are LIGHT in Yahuah. Live as children of LIGHT - for the fruit of the light consists in all goodness, righteousness and truth - and find out what pleases Yahuah. Have nothing to do with the fruitless deeds of darkness, but rather expose them." - Ephesians 5:8-12
Find out what pleases Yahuah, your Creator.
Obedience is praised *if it fits traditional norms*, but condemned *if it fits Scriptural instructions*. Scripture is divided, and a division exists between the Hebrew / Yahudi (Jew) and the Gentile Christian in terms of what is to be obeyed or ignored in the Torah, based on this difference. So, in their teachings, there is not one body of believers, although this will be denied by most.
The word, Christianity, is not found anywhere in Scripture.
Why do we pretend it is? Encyclopedias tell us it is a *religion*, and that it was founded by *Jesus Christ*. It was really founded by Simon Magus, and his tomb is under the altar in St. Peter's Cathedral at

Rome. No follower of Yahusha ever taught us anything about Sunday, Easter, Christmas, popes, nuns, holy water, sacraments, or any separation of Yahusha's body into a priesthood and laity. We are ALL priests on level ground with one another, and He is our High Priest. If you are studying something, and embrace it as a way of living, shouldn't you search it out completely and find where its roots lead? If the root is good, then the fruit it bears will also be good.
Christianity is a usurper, and a religion without Hebrew roots; it grew from pagan Greco-Latin roots.

ABORTION - A CHILD'S VIEWPOINT
There's a way to meet the child you destroyed:
Get Torahfied before Yahusha returns

ABORTION: A CHILD'S VIEWPOINT

DEAR MOMMY:

I SEE YOU SMILING, BUT WITH TEARS.
I'D LOVE TO BE THERE BY YOUR SIDE.
BUT BY YOUR CHOICE, I VIEW FROM ABOVE.
TELL MY GRANDPARENTS I SEND MY LOVE.
IT'S BEAUTIFUL HERE; IS ALL I CAN SAY.
YOUR LIFE CAN GO ON WITHOUT ME BEING IN YOUR WAY.
I LOVE YOU MOMMY!
THERE'S A WAY TO MEET THE CHILD YOU DESTROYED

GET TORAHFIED
BEFORE YAHUSHA RETURNS

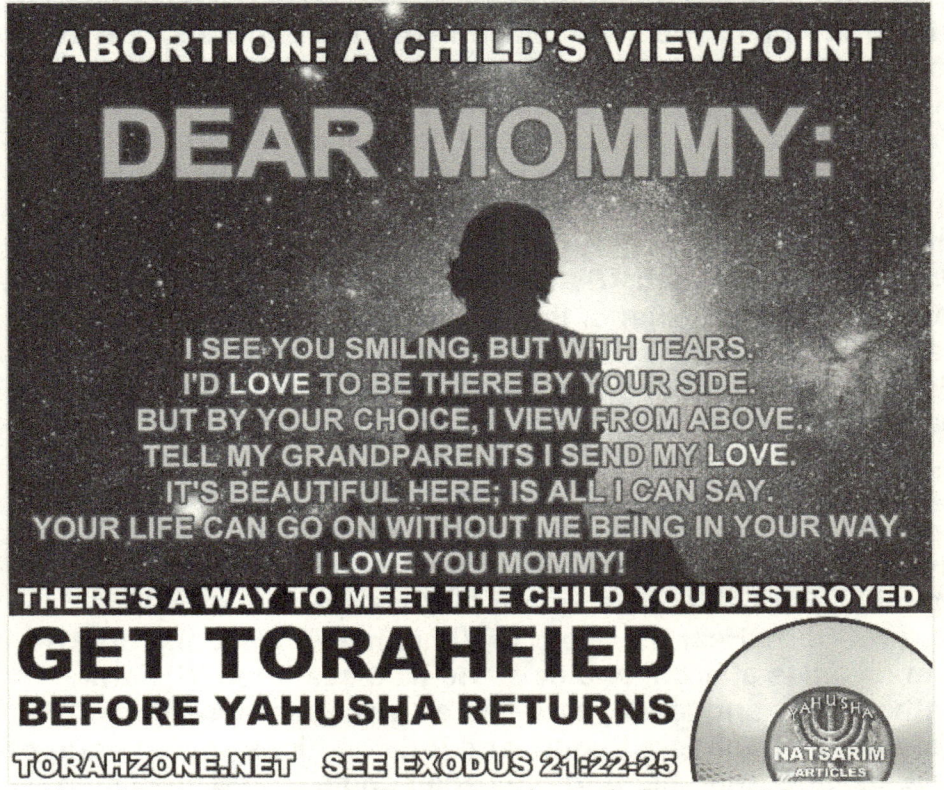

TORAHZONE.NET   SEE EXODUS 21:22-25

Use this data source to learn, teach, and share – 100+ tracts
NATSARIM AMBASSADOR DISC

The following is rarely taught in its entirety.

The wolves don't want you to awaken to what it reveals. It tells us the **Natsarim** will cry-out a final message, and you will see why the nations rage. Pay close attention; it unmasks the lies.
Yahuah is looking for His obedient wife, the maiden, His ashah.

YIRMEYAHU (Jeremiah, *Yahuah uplifts*)
Chapter 31:1-40:
"'At that time,' says Yahuah, 'I shall be the Alahim of all the clans of Yisharal, and they shall be My people.' Thus said Yahuah, 'A people escaped from the sword found favor in the wilderness, Yisharal, when it went to find rest.' Yahuah appeared to me from afar, saying, 'I have loved you with an everlasting love, therefore I shall draw you with kindness. I am going to build you again. And you shall be rebuilt, O maiden of Yisharal! Again, you shall take up your tambourines, and go forth in the dances of those who rejoice. Again, you shall plant vines on the mountains of Shamarun.
The planters shall plant and treat them as common.
For there shall be a yom when the Natsarim cry on Mount Afrayim, "Arise, and let us go up to Tsiun, to Yahuah our Alahim."
For thus said Yahuah, 'Sing with gladness for Yaqub, and shout among the chief of the guyim. Cry out, give praise, and say, "Yahuah, save Your people, the remnant of Yisharal!" See, I am bringing them from the land of the north, and shall gather them from the ends of the arets, among them the blind and the lame, those with child and those in labor, together – a great assembly returning here. With weeping they shall come, and with their prayers I bring them. I shall make them walk by rivers of mayim, in a straight way in which they do not stumble. For I shall be a Father to Yisharal, and Afrayim – he is My first-born. Hear the Word of Yahuah, O guyim, and declare it in the isles afar off, and say, "He who scattered Yisharal gathers him, and shall guard him as a shepherd his flock." For Yahuah shall ransom Yaqub, and redeem him from the hand of one stronger than he. And they shall come in and shall sing on the height of Tsiun, and stream to the goodness of Yahuah, for grain and for new wine and for oil, and for the young of the flock and the herd. And their being shall be like a well-watered garden, and never languish again. Then shall a maiden rejoice

in a dance, and young men and old, together. And I shall turn their mourning to joy, and shall comfort them, and shall make them rejoice from their sorrow, and shall fill the being of the priests with fatness. And My people shall be satisfied with My goodness,' says Yahuah.

Thus said Yahuah, 'A voice was heard in Ramah, wailing, bitter weeping, Rakel weeping for her children, refusing to be comforted for her children, because they are no more.' Thus said Yahuah, 'Hold back your voice from weeping, and your eyes from tears, for there is a reward for your work,' says Yahuah, 'and they shall return from the land of the enemy. And there is expectancy for your latter end,' says Yahuah, 'and your children shall return to their own country. I have clearly heard Afrayim lamenting, "You have chastised me, and I was chastised, like an untrained calf. Turn me back, and I shall turn back, for You are Yahuah my Alahim. For after my turning back, I repented. And after I was instructed, I struck myself on the thigh. I was ashamed, even humiliated, for I bore the reproach of my youth." Is Afrayim a precious son to Me, a child of delights? For though I spoke against him, I still remembered him. That is why My affections were deeply moved for him. I have great compassion for him,' says Yahuah. 'Set up signposts, make landmarks; set your heart toward the highway, the way in which you went. Turn back, O maiden of Yisharal, turn back to these cities of yours! Till when would you turn here and there, O backsliding daughter? For Yahuah has created what is new on arets: an ashah encompasses a man!' Thus said Yahuah Tsabauth, the Alahim of Yisharal, 'Let them once again say this word in the land of Yahudah and in its cities, when I turn back their captivity, "Yahuah bless you, O home of obedience, mountain of qodeshness!" And in Yahudah and all its cities farmers and those who journey with flocks, shall dwell together. For I shall fill the weary being, and I shall replenish every grieved being.' At this I awoke and looked around, and my sleep was sweet to me. 'See, the Yomim are coming,' says Yahuah, 'that I shall sow the house of Yisharal and the house of Yahudah with the seed of man and the seed of beast. And it shall be, that as I have watched over them to pluck up, and to break down, and to throw down, and to destroy, and to afflict, so I shall watch over them to build and to plant,' says Yahuah. 'In those Yomim they shall no longer say, "The fathers ate sour grapes, and the children's teeth are blunted." But each one shall die for his own lawlessness – whoever eats sour grapes, his teeth shall be blunted. See, the Yomim are coming,' says Yahuah, 'when I shall make a renewed Covenant with the house of Yisharal and with the house of Yahudah, not like the covenant I made with their fathers in the yom when I took them by the hand to bring them out of the land of Mitsrim, My Covenant which they broke, though I was a Husband to them,' says Yahuah. For this is the Covenant I shall make with the house of Yisharal after those Yomim,' says Yahuah: 'I shall put My Turah in their inward parts, and write it on their hearts. And I shall be their Alahim, and they shall be My people. And no longer shall they teach, each one his neighbor, and each one his brother, saying, "Know Yahuah," for they shall all know Me, from the least of them to the greatest of them,' says Yahuah. 'For I shall forgive their lawlessness, and remember their sin no more.' Thus said Yahuah, who gives the Sun for a light by yom, and the laws of the Moon and the stars for a light by lailah, who stirs up the sea, and its waves roar – Yahuah Tsabauth is His Name: 'If these laws vanish from before Me,' says Yahuah, 'then the seed of Yisharal shall also cease from being a nation before Me forever.' Thus said Yahuah, 'If the shamayim above could be measured, and the foundations of the arets searched out beneath, I would also cast off all the seed of Yisharal for all that they have done,' says Yahuah. 'See, the Yomim are coming,' says Yahuah, 'that the city shall be built for Yahuah from the Tower of Kananal to the Corner Gate. And the measuring line shall again extend straight ahead to the hill Gareb, then it shall turn toward Goah. And all the valley of the dead bodies and of the ashes, and all the fields as far as the wadi Qidron, to the corner of the Horse Gate toward the east, is to be qodesh to Yahuah. It shall not be plucked up or thrown down any more forever.'" - YirmeYahu (Jer.) 31:1-40 BYNV

Context reveals the fullest meaning, so I will end this book with the wise words of Shalomoh, the man of peace. The books of Scripture are often named for the first word or phrase in them, and the one

known since the 14th century as **Ecclesiates** (Greek word from ecclesia, for congregation, assembly) is **QOHELETH**.
This word in Eberith (Hebrew) literally means **assembly man.**
Digest the idioms *(figurative speech, abstract expressions).*
Read it slowly, and notice what it leads us to guard, and watch over carefully. Yahuah is serious about His ashah, and wants her clean, unwrinkled, obedient, and loving. We can choose the best, and live forever; or *'we can choose second-best, **or worse.**'* [quote, Ray Todd]
Most of the time, people give Yahuah their second-best, or worse. Yahuah deserves better, He gives us His best eternally. Read the words of Yahuah at YirmeYahu (Jer.) 29:10-14:

"For thus said Yahuah, 'When 70 years are completed, at Babel I shall visit you and establish My good word toward you, to bring you back to this place. For I know the plans I am planning for you,' says Yahuah, 'plans of peace and not of evil, to give you a future and an expectancy. Then you shall call on Me, and shall come and pray to Me, and I shall listen to you. And you shall seek Me, and shall find Me, when you search for Me with all your heart. And I shall be found by you,' says Yahuah, 'and I shall turn back your captivity, and shall gather you from all the guyim and from all the places where I have driven you, says Yahuah. And I shall bring you back to the place from which I have exiled you.'"

Yahusha is the Way, the Truth, and the Life, and these *living words* were *breathed* into us. He is the Light of mankind, the Maker:

QOHELETH (Ecclesiates, *assembly man*) **12:1-14 – BYNV**
Please note the idioms:

"**Remember** also your Creator in the Yomim of your youth, before the evil Yomim come, and the years draw near when you say,
"I have no pleasure in them."
Before the Sun and the light, the Moon and the stars, are darkened, [eyesight fails] and the clouds return after the rain [foggy mind];
in the yom [day] when the guards of the house tremble [hands quake], and the strong men shall bow down [legs fail]; when the grinders shall cease because they are few [dental troubles], and those that look through the windows shall become dim [eyesight fails further]; and the doors shall be shut in the streets, and the sound of grinding is low [hearing problems]; and one rises up at the sound of a bird [trouble

sleeping], and all the daughters of song are bowed down [voice fails]; furthermore, they are afraid of what is high, and of low places in the way; and the almond tree blossoms [hair changes], and the grasshopper becomes a burden [any labor is difficult], and desire perishes [libido fails]. For man is going to his everlasting home, and the mourners shall go about the streets. Remember Him before the silver cord is loosed, or the golden bowl is broken, or the jar shattered at the fountain, or the wheel broken at the well, and the dust returns to the arets as it was, and the ruach returns to Alahim Who gave it. *"Futility! Futility!"* said the Qoheleth, *"All is futile."*
And besides being wise, Qoheleth also taught the people knowledge, and he listened and sought out – set in order many proverbs. Qoheleth sought to find out words of delight, and words of truth, rightly written.
The words of the wise are like goads, and as nails driven by Adunim of collections – they were given by one Shepherd.
And besides these, my son, *be warned – the making of many books has no end,* and much study is a wearying of the flesh.
Let us hear the conclusion of the entire matter:
Fear Alahim and guard His commands, for this applies to all mankind! For Alahim shall bring every work into lawfulness, including all that is hidden, whether good or whether evil."

    Obey the Commandments; they teach mankind how to love.
    Love one another: the physical world is an empire of dust.
    The real world is eternal, and we want you there.
    Come with us, and come out of the mother of harlots.

GLOSSARY
Hebrew Transliterations
And English Definitions

Important note: This is a partial listing of Hebrew / Eberith transliterations and definitions. Meanings are determined by the *context* of the word. How a word is used in a sentence helps us discern how to apply a proper definition. A pitcher can mean more than one thing, and Hebrew words can too.
At the end of this glossary is a *letter comparison chart*.
The context supplies a word's meaning in a sentence.
A common error of many students and teachers is to consult a concordance and select a definition on a whim. The meanings a word may have must not be applied mindlessly without taking the context into account. Natsarim are being restored to a clean lip.

Ab, Abba [alef-beth]   Father, male head of household, strong protector

Abrahim …. Abram or AbuRamu (exalted father) renamed by Yahuah: Abrahim - father of nations or father of multitudes

Adam ….   Man, mankind, human, humanity, Earthling; created with a shared essence / character with Yahuah, in order to **rule over** creation; depending on the context, it can also mean red

Aduni ….   Hebrew for *my lord* or *my sovereign*. Commonly seen transliterated *Adonai*.

Afraim …. Second son of Yusef, received blessing of first-born. His name means *fruitful.* Commonly spelled *Ephraim*

Al, Alah ….   Al, Alah, Alahim are pronouns meaning the mighty, high, or lofty one. The plural ending can refer to the majesty, or power of the One. Commonly we see the spelling **El**, or **Elohim** due to the distortions of vowels (niqqud marks) invented by the Masoretes, Karaite **traditionalists. Masorah** means tradition. The Karaite sect was founded by Anan Ben Daud in the 8th century CE. There are no such marks found prior to the 8th century, so the Dead Sea Scrolls were found without them.

The first letter in the word Alahim is **ALEF**; an **A**, not an **E**. Al is pronounced *ALL*. Yahuah has hidden the sound of His original Speech in a most unexpected place: Arabic-Hebrew.

Those who are concerned that EL, and ALAH have been used as **proper nouns** by pagans should distinguish between the difference between a **NAME**, and a **clean Hebrew word** that is a **pronoun**. Other cultures have picked up many clean Hebrew words and turned them into names, such as Aman, Adon, and Molok. When not used as **names**, these terms are authentic, clean words.

The descendants of Abrahim through Yishmaal were not attacked and carried into all the world, but continue **to utter the old form** of many Hebrew words, since they ARE **Hebrews**. They refer to their mighty-one as **allah**, which they know is not a name, but simply means god, as they explain it to English-speaking people today. The term itself **is original**; but **their** allah is not **our Alah, Yahuah**, since **their** allah does not have a son, and they do not obey Yahuah's Covenant. Many other words are preserved on the Masoretes. Arabic/Hebrew from *the other side of the family* preserves the original sound of words such as Abram, Daud, Yusef, Yaqub, Aishah, dam, Iason, etc. The Arabic/Hebrew word for mother, *um*, closely resembles the modern Hebrew *em* [vowel-trouble again]. The Arabic/Hebrew for father, *ab*, is more correct than the modern Hebrew, *av*, since there was not a letter "**V**" in ancient Hebrew (Eberith).

Am, Ama [alef-mem] Mother, female term, one giving birth, nurturer; EM [ayin-mem] means *people*. AM means *mother*

Aman .... 3 Hebrew letters, alef-mem-nun: **AMN**; Meaning: affirmation; *truly, trusted.*
The femine form is *amanah*, found in Scripture translations as faith, but means trustworthy. Both aman and amanah refer to the idea of being **trustworthy** and **truthful**.
This word is **not in any way** related to the Egyptian deity AMEN or AMON RA.
The word AMON is the **Greek form** of the Egyptian word **YAMANU**, which meant the *hidden-one*. There is no relationship or contextual connection between the Hebrew use of the word aman with the Greek or Egyptian languages. People are hearing things that aren't there, therefore they are being deluded / mesmerized by false

teachings. Proverbs 14:15 tells us how a simpleton believes everything he hears, but a prudent person checks things.

Arets .... Earth, soil, land

Ash, Ashah ... Man, Woman - male: *ash*; female: *ashah*

Asherah ... tree idol   plural: Asherim Seen today in the Christmas tree, a phallus depicting gonads (orbs) and semen (tinsel)

Astoreth ... plural of Astoreth, Philistine deity; aka Astarte; equivalent to Eostre, Eastre, Easter, Isis, Ishtar

BEL (Baal) .... Lord, master, owner; a word adopted as a proper noun (name) for the Kanaanite storm deity BEL, in Hebrew it is spelled beth-ayin-lamed. Plural form: *Baalim*

Behemah .... A beast, living creature; plural: BEHEMOTH The plural may refer to a single beast of a great size. Certain plural endings in Hebrew pertain to quantity, but in some cases the quality of strength or size. Also used as a metaphor for the principalities controlling and ruling mankind (clergy, nobility, and laity), given power and authority by the dragon.
A more modern term is *beast*: a giant monster (World Order).

Besorah .... Message, testimony, report

CONSONANT: A consonant is a letter making use of the lips, teeth, upper teeth on lower lip, or tongue on the roof of the mouth.
VOWEL: A vowel is a letter sounded without using the lips, teeth, upper teeth on lower lip, or tongue on the roof of the mouth; only the breath and mouth cavity are used.
Knowing this, the form often heard for the Name, "YEHO*V*AH" is an obvious error which teachers have inherited from one another.

First-fruits .... This is a shadow or outline using the waving of barley during the week of Matsah, or Unleavened Bread. Following Passover, we see the sign of Yunah because Yahusha's resurrection is the redemptive shadow showing Him to be the First-fruits. It's really not about barley at all, the barley was simply the shadow; Yahusha's resurrection is the reality

Guyim .... Plural form of guy, meaning gentiles, nations, who are to engraft to Yisharal by pledging in immersion, to the Covenant; then treated the same as native-born, no dividing wall; same Turah applies

Hekal .... Temple, Shrine - House built by Shalomoh, destroyed by Babylonians, rebuilt 70 years later, after return from Babel under governor, NekemYah. Koresh ordered and paid for the rebuilding.

Kanukah .... Dedication (aka Chanukah, Hanukkah)

Kerem   Vine, vineyard, or garden

The Hebrew word for vineyard is *KEREM*. This word is spelled with three letters in the original Eberith (Hebrew) script:
Kaf-resh-mem (please see letter chart)

Yahusha is the KEREM (Vine), and we are His NATSARIM meaning *branches, watchmen, or guardians*

Kodesh   Renewed month, cycle, *period of time* (see QODESH)

Kohen .... Hebrew word for priest; plural *kohenim*
The meaning is friend, worker, minister, server.
Cognate words include kahuna, kahin, king, koehn, kohn, cohn; revealing how the word is synonymous with many statements about us becoming kings and priests under Yahusha, our Kohen haGadol (the High Priest)

Kuram-Abi: *Named a 2Khronicles 2:13* - A Tyrain man of the tribe of Dan filled with wisdom and skill. In their drive to promote Reason as the highest goal, modern Masonry's Adepts refer to this man as they seek vengeance against 3 allegorical conspirators they claim slew Huram: government, religion, and private property – Marxist philosophy embracing Secular Humanism, situation ethics, athieism, and communism [New World Order, New Age, the worship of Reason]

Lailah .... Night, darkness

Lui .... The name of the father of the tribe of priests; plural form Luim Commonly seen as LEVI, LEVITE; Aharon and Mosheh were Luim

Malakim .... Messengers; singular form: malak, "angel"

Mayim .... Water, waters

Miqra .... Proclamation; root *qara*, to proclaim. The quran is the Hebrew term used by Muslims for Mohammad's words.
The Karaites derive the name for their sect from QARA.

Mishkan .. Temple, Dwelling Place

Moed .... Appointment; plural form: moedim

Molok .... Kananim / Moabim deity also known as Rephan, Kemosh to Amonites, Kiyyun, Tophet, etc.,. Children were offered alive to pass through the fire as offerings to this abomination – Nimrod was known among the nations by all sorts of babbled terms.

Mosheh .... *Draw out* - Hebrew spelling: MEM-SHIN-HAY

Nefesh .... Breath, blast, living spirit, life-giving essence, cognate with nehash (breathe), and nekash (hiss).
Often translated *soul,* inner being, strong man, psyche.

Qodesh .... *Set-apart* (not KODESH, a word for month)

Ruach ... Breath, wind, breeze, also known as "spirit"

Sefer .... Scroll, book (Greco-Latin: cepher)

Shabua .... Week, from root *sheba*, seven; plural form: *Shabuoth* (weeks)

Shabuoth .... Plural form of shabua: *weeks*. The event memorialized as the marriage Covenant between Yahuah and Yisharal. The anniversary of the marriage Covenant is annually observed on the 50th day after First-fruits, and is always on the first day of the week, the "morrow after the seventh Shabath."

Shalomoh .... Peaceful, Man of peace, son of Daud

Shamash .... Servant; context may refer to the visible object called the Sun, or the adopted name for the deity pagans called on to worship the Sun.

The context supplies a word's intended meaning in a sentence. A common error of many students and teachers is to consult a concordance, and select a definition on a whim. The meanings a word may have must not be applied mindlessly without discerning the context.

Shamayim .... Skies, heavens

Sheol .... Abode of the dead, **the grave**, commonly termed hell, meaning *hole* - This is not the same as the Lake of Fire, *Yam Aish*

Talmid .... Student, pupil; plural form, talmidim

Turah .... Instruction; plural form *Turoth*

Tsabaoth .... Armies; tsaba (army) + plural ending, *oth*

Tsedek .... Upright, righteous

Tsitsith .... Tassels (purplish-blue in color, see Num. 15, Dt. 22). They are worn on our garments to remind us to obey the Instructions of Torah always.

VOWEL: A vowel is a letter sounded without using the lips, teeth, upper teeth on lower lip, or tongue on the roof of the mouth; only the breath and mouth cavity are used.
CONSONANT: A consonant is a letter making use of the lips, teeth, upper teeth on lower lip, or tongue on the roof of the mouth. Knowing this, the form often heard for the Name, "YEHO<u>V</u>AH" is an obvious error which teachers have inherited from one another.

Yahuah   *four vowels,* Tetragrammaton: **yod-hay-uau-hay**. The Personal Name of our Creator, meaning: I will be there;
I was, I am, I will be

Yahusha .... Name of Mashiak, means: *Yah (I am) your Deliverer*

Yam, Yamim .... Sea, seas

Yam Aish ... Lake of fire, place of permanent, utter destruction; this is the second death

Yerak .... Moon (the visible object of the Moon we see)

Yashar .... Upright, just, level, straight (unrelated to the next word)

Yisharal .... Ruler with Alahim; **Shar** (the root, *rule*) means prince, ruler; seen today in terms such as sheriff, sharif. The letter Y is a prefix meaning to, and the suffix AL refers to Alahim. The meaning is *"to rule with Alahim."* Many define it as *to struggle* (wrestle) *with Alahim*. This elect group is often referred to in Scripture as the bride or ashah of Yahuah, the one body in Covenant with Him. Guyim, or foreigners, **must** become engrafted, or perish without hope. Those ingrafted are to be treated as the native-born. Ruth did this, being a former Moabitess, and became the great-grandmother of Daud, and named in the geneaology of Yahusha.

All who accept the Renewed Covenant through the covering of Yahusha's blood (trusting in His offering, not the blood of animals), must be immersed as the outward sign of their pledge / commitment to obedience. This seals them as Yahusha's elect for the Day of our redemption. By learning Yahuah's Covenant of love, every person is convicted of transgressing His instructions. Yahusha's perfect offering of His own blood redeems completely. There remains to more offering for sins. The hand-writing that was against us is wiped clean (the list of our sins). They are forgotten, and His blood redeems us. Through the process of being convicted in our heart that we need Him, we repent (turn back), and pledge to obey Yahuah's instructions in His power as we call on the Name of Deliverance for the forgiveness of sin: Yahusha. He is our Rock and our Redeemer.

Yom, Yomim .... Day, days

Yusef .... Son of Yaqub, father of Afraim (Ephraim) & Menashah; distorted by letters & vowels of gentile languages as Joseph.
The name means *he who adds*.

Zonah .... cult / shrine prostitute

All this author's eBooks are enabled for Text-to-Speech
Alexa can read them to you

DO YOU WANT THE BYNV?

Amazon has it. The BYNV is available as a Kindle eBook, or in printed form. It had to be split into two volumes because Amazon cannot print it as one book, they have a page-number limitation. The world needs to read the Word of Yahuah, so it will be available anywhere in the world, printed near to those who order it, with free shipping to those with Amazon Prime.

Amazon site for shirts endorsed by the author:
Yahusha World Garments

AVAILABLE WORLD-WIDE FROM AMAZON.COM

Amazon Books & eBooks

**THE WORDS OF THE FIRST NATSARIM (BELOW LEFT)
BOTH TRANSLATED INTO ENGLISH BY ONE OF THE LAST NATSARIM:**

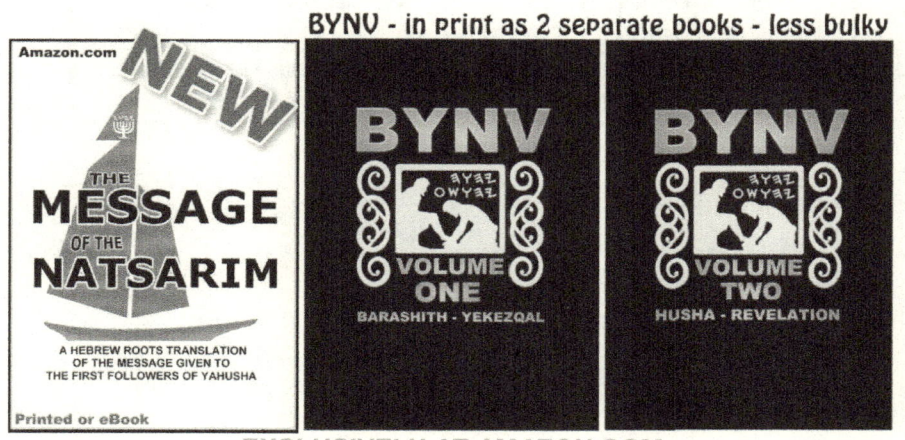

BYNV - in print as 2 separate books - less bulky

Amazon.com **NEW**
THE **MESSAGE** OF THE **NATSARIM**
A HEBREW ROOTS TRANSLATION
OF THE MESSAGE GIVEN TO
THE FIRST FOLLOWERS OF YAHUSHA
Printed or eBook

BYNV VOLUME ONE
BARASHITH - YEKEZQAL

BYNV VOLUME TWO
HUSHA - REVELATION

EXCLUSIVELY AT AMAZON.COM

MASHIAK OR ANTI-MASHIAK

YAHUSHA WOULD NOT BE MASHIAK IF HE ALTERED COMMANDMENTS OR FAILED TO OBEY AND TEACH THEM

TRUE MASHIAK	ANTI-MASHIAK
LIVED BY AND TAUGHT TORAH & FESTIVALS	MAN OF SIN "LAWLESS ONE"
OBSERVED SHABATH ATE ONLY FOOD SET-APART BY WORD CAME IN FATHER'S NAME	FOLLOWERS CLAIM TORAH IS "DONE AWAY" & CHANGED TORAH EAT THE UNCLEAN PROFANE SHABATH
YAHUSHA SPOKE HIS FATHER'S WORDS	**JESUS** ANOTHER'S NAME: ZEUS

DO NOT ADD OR TAKE AWAY FROM THE WORD OF YAHUAH, LIVE BY EVERY WORD THAT PROCEEDS FROM THE MOUTH OF YAHUAH

TORAH INSTITUTE   TORAHZONE.NET   DT. 4:2

LETTER CHART – HEBREW, LATIN, GREEK:

LETTER CHART

LATIN		HEBREW	ARAMAIC			GREEK	
A	alef	⩺	א	1	ox	alpha	A
B	beth	ϑ	ב	2	house	beta	B
G	gimel	٦	ג	3	camel	gamma	Γ
D	daleth	Δ	ד	4	door	delta	Δ
H	hay	ᶟ	ה	5	window	hoi	H
U	uau	Y	ו	6	hook	**upsilon**	Y
Z	zayin	Ζ	ז	7	weapon	zeta	Z
CH	heth	Ħ	ח	8	fence	(h)eta	H
T	teth	⊗	ט	9	winding	theta	Θ
Y	yod	ʓ	׳	10	hand	iota	I
K	kaph	ע	כ	20	bent hand	kappa	K
L	lamed	⌒	ל	30	goad	lambda	Λ
M	mem	ᴍ	מ	40	water	mu	M
N	nun	ע	נ	50	fish	nu	N
S	samek	⟊	ס	60	prop	xei	Ξ
E/A	ayin	O	ע	70	eye	omega	Ω
P	pe	⌐	פ	80	mouth	pei	Π
TS	tsadee	⊢	צ	90	hook	zeta	Z
Q	koph	Ϙ	ק	100	needle eye	chi	X
R	resh	◁	ר	200	head	rho	P
SH	shin	W	ש	300	tooth	sigma	Σ
T	tau	✕	ת	400	mark	tau	T

TO THE FIRST AND THE LAST NATSARIM:
THE REVELATION OF YAHUSHA

"'I am the Alef and the Tau (alef-tau) Beginning and End,' says Yahuah, 'Who is and Who was and Who is to come, the Almighty.'" (Al Shaddai)
Revelation 1:8

"And when I saw Him, I fell at His feet as dead, and He placed His right hand on me, saying, 'Do not be afraid, I am the First and the Last, and the living One. And I became dead, and see, I am living forever and ever, Aman. And I possess the keys of the grave and of death. Write therefore what you have seen, both what is now and what shall take place after these.'"
Revelation 1:17-19

And His Name is called
Wonder, Counsellor, Strong Al, Father of Continuity, Prince of Peace.

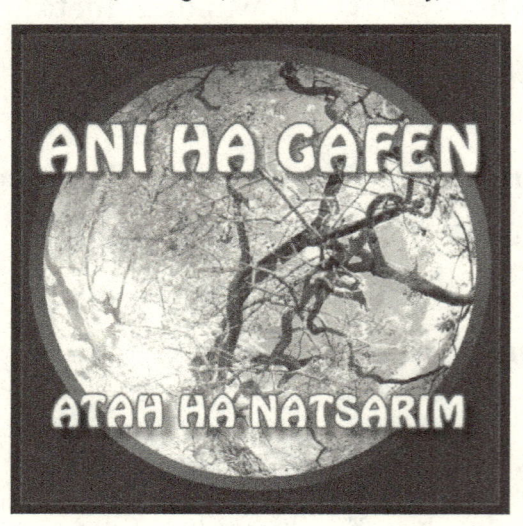

ANI HA GAFEN

ATAH HA NATSARIM

"I am the Vine, you are the Natsarim"

Made in the USA
Monee, IL
20 April 2021